Warfare & Weaponry in
in
Dynastic Egypt

For Kevin, Ingrid, and Charlotte Dean. There are not enough ways in which I can say thank you.

Warfare & Weaponry in Dynastic Egypt

Rebecca Dean

PEN & SWORD
ARCHAEOLOGY

First published in Great Britain in 2017 by
PEN & SWORD ARCHAEOLOGY
an imprint of
Pen & Sword Books Ltd,
47 Church Street,
Barnsley,
South Yorkshire.
S70 2AS

A CIP record for this book is available from the British Library.

ISBN 978 1 47382 355 6

Printed and bound in the UK
by TJ International Ltd

Pen & Sword Books Ltd incorporates the Imprints of
Pen & Sword Aviation, Pen & Sword Maritime,
Pen & Sword Military, Wharncliffe Local History, Pen & Sword Select, Pen
& Sword Military Classics and Leo Cooper.

For a complete list of Pen & Sword titles please contact
Pen & Sword Books Limited
47 Church Street, Barnsley, South Yorkshire, S70 2AS, England
E-mail: enquiries@pen-and-sword.co.uk
Website: www.pen-and-sword.co.uk

Content

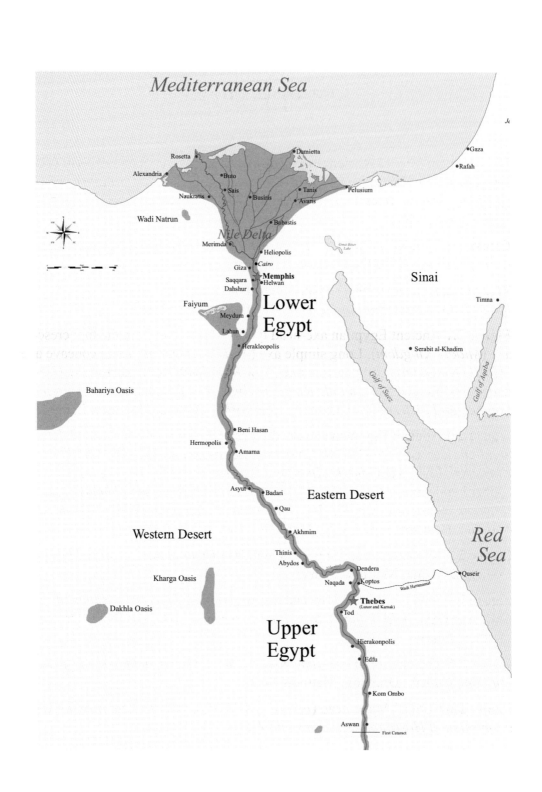

List of Figures

- **Figure A.11:** Mace-head (*Photo: R A Dean, produced here with the kind permission of Harrogate Museum and Arts*)

- **Figure A.12:** Mace-head (*Photo: R A Dean, produced here with the kind permission of Harrogate Museum and Arts*)

- **Figure A.13:** Mace-head (*Photo: R A Dean, produced here with the kind permission of Harrogate Museum and Arts*)

- **Figure A.14:** Mace-head (*Photo: R A Dean, produced here with the kind permission of Harrogate Museum and Arts*)

- **Figure A.15:** Mace-head (*Photo: R A Dean, produced here with the kind permission of Harrogate Museum and Arts*)

- **Figure A.16:** Mace-head (*Photo: R A Dean, produced here with the kind permission of Harrogate Museum and Arts*)

- **Figure A.17:** Mace-head (*Photo: R A Dean, produced here with the kind permission of Harrogate Museum and Arts*)

Acknowledgements

While writing this book I have had no end of support and encouragement from some amazing people.

Professor Joann Fletcher was a wonderful help as my tutor at the University of York and her infectious enthusiasm for all things Egypt really inspired my work both at university and here. I will be forever grateful to her for all her encouragement and championing of my work.

Gemma Harker, editor extraordinaire, my dearest friend and my constant cheerleader; I cannot thank her enough for all her help.

Matthew Leary, an amazing artist whose contribution to this book cannot be overstated; his exquisite drawings have really lifted this book to new heights.

Dr Lucy Wilson, my friend and flatmate for nearly ten years; she always found my work fascinating, no matter how weird it got (and thanks again for putting up with the pig skull stored in the bath for two weeks).

Dr Katie Tyreman-Herrington, a fellow postgraduate at York; she never failed to cheer me up and gave me constant support and advice.

William Stonborough, a fellow York Egyptology student; his fascinating work has been so important to my understanding of defence in ancient Egypt.

Professor Loveday Alexander who has always been interested in my work and has unceasingly excellent counsel and guidance readily available.

The Raval family, who are wonderful friends and supporters (and suppliers of excellent whisky).

Sarah Rogers, a close friend for so many years; she has always been strong advocate for using my research for education.

The choir of St Philip and St James, Alderley Edge; they kept me relatively sane when my work threatened to completely overwhelm me.

The girls of HGHC (you know who you are!).

My family, the Dean clan (English and Welsh branches!); they are the most amazing and supportive family a girl could ask for.

And finally Eleri; for walking all over my keyboard and thereby contributing her own unique additions to the book (whether I wanted her to or not).

Any errors apparent in this book are mine, and mine alone.

Simple Chronology of Ancient Egypt

Predynastic Egypt
(pre-3100 BC)

Early Dynastic Period
(First – Second Dynasties; c.3100 BC – c.2686 BC)

The Old Kingdom
(Third – Sixth Dynasties; c.2686 BC – c.2181 BC)

First Intermediate Period
(Seventh – Eleventh Dynasties; c.2181 BC – c.2055 BC)

The Middle Kingdom
(Twelfth – Thirteenth Dynasties; c.2055 BC – c.1650 BC)

Second Intermediate Period
(Fourteenth – Seventeenth Dynasties; c.1650 BC – c.1550 BC)

The New Kingdom
(Eighteenth – Twentieth Dynasties; c.1550 BC – c.1077 BC)

Third Intermediate Period
(Twenty-First– Twenty-Fifth Dynasties; c.1077 BC – c.664 BC)

Late Period
(Twenty-Sixth – Thirty-First Dynasties; c.664 BC – c.332 BC)

Graeco-Roman Period
(332 BC – 619 AD)

Introduction

I have had a life-long fascination with ancient warfare and weaponry, as well as with ancient Egypt, so studying ancient Egyptian warfare was pretty much all of my dreams come true. This obsession with ancient Egyptian warfare was nurtured first by my remarkably understanding parents and later by a wonderful tutor at university. My meandering path through my university years eventually led to the writing of this book.

There can be no doubt that warfare in ancient Egypt is a well-studied subject. There has always been a fascination with how early societies conducted their wars and ancient Egypt is no exception. The research has been wide-ranging and certain aspects of ancient Egyptian warfare have been examined comprehensively. The potential reasons as to why the ancient Egyptians went to war have been looked at in great detail academically, along with the structure and composition of the ancient Egyptian military. There has also been a great deal of work done on events, such as the Battle of Kadesh, along with detailed studies of the various weapons that were in use throughout the Dynastic period.

Through this book I am aiming to provide a new way of looking at ancient Egyptian weapons and warfare. Firstly, we will look closely at the history and developments of warfare throughout ancient Egypt, before focusing on the composition and varying styles of weapons which were used during the millennia of Dynastic Egypt. From their earliest forms in the very beginnings of the united ancient Egyptian state to the elaborate and more technologically advanced weapons influenced by the very history of Dynastic Egypt, the weapons are a subject of much fascination.

The evidence for warfare and weaponry in ancient Egypt is compelling and wide-ranging, with a combination of artefactual, visual, and textual evidence contributing to our understanding of the subject. Whilst there are a lot of different pieces of evidence for the warlike pharaohs, literary descriptions of soldiers training and daily duties make for intriguing little insights into the non-royal participants in ancient Egyptian warfare. The same can be said for the various reliefs of the 'warrior pharaoh' – if you look to the side of the god-like image of the pharaoh you will sometimes see images of his soldiers and their enemies in the heat of battle. Finally, weapons burials can provide a great deal of information regarding the sort of weaponry used by the pharaohs and by other ancient Egyptians. If all of this evidence is collated and used together we can learn a great deal about ancient

Egyptian warfare. Sometimes it seems that not enough work is done examining all the potential pieces of evidence together, looking at the whole picture, so to say. The minutia of Egyptian archaeology is fascinating, but it is worth taking a step back every now and then.

Weapons, while interesting, are of little use on their own, so it is also important that we look at the lives (and deaths) of people who made use of these weapons, all with varying degrees of success. Here we will look at both the pictorial evidence which can be seen in carvings and reliefs, as well as the physical remains of both soldiers and civilians who were injured during combat. On occasion we even will be able to look at contemporary written accounts of battles and executions.

A particular focus of this book will be a relatively unexplored area of the wider field of weapons and warfare in ancient Egypt: the involvement of ancient Egyptian women. I have spent a great deal of time examining this specific aspect of ancient Egyptian warfare and have been surprised and amazed by the range of evidence which has been systematically ignored or interpreted with great cultural bias. Figures such as Hatshepsut, Nefertiti, and Tawosret are wonderful examples of ancient Egyptian women who used weapons and/or took part in warfare to some extent. As well as these extreme examples we will also have a look at the, probably more commonplace, idea of women taking up arms to defend their town while their men-folk were away. Such women are an important part of ancient Egyptian history and are equally relevant in this modern age, where questions about women taking part in combat in active war-zones are still being asked in the modern military of several countries.

Finally, and of particular interest to me, will be an exploration of the possibilities for experimental archaeology, both as a method of testing out the weaponry and as a way of discovering more about the weapons themselves through the active process of using them. Extensive work on this subject has been carried out by both myself and a postgraduate contemporary of mine at the University of York, William Stonborough, and the detailed information we have gleaned about weapons trauma will be examined here. Such evidence allows us to reconstruct more fully which weapons were used in combat and how they may have been constructed and wielded.

My aim is to take you through the rich history that is the development of warfare and weaponry in Dynastic Egypt, summarising the most interesting and relevant pieces of previous research as well as highlighting the latest evidence. Through a mixture of academic study and experimental research I have gained a detailed understanding of weaponry and warfare in ancient Egyptian history which I would like to share with you. I hope you enjoy reading about ancient Egypt's military past as much as I enjoyed researching it.

1

Warfare in Ancient Egypt

Weaponry and warfare is a subject that has a long-held fascination for many people. For me, it is an interest that began in childhood and continued unabated into adulthood and university life. The research I carried out concentrated not only on ancient Egyptian warfare, but on the several examples of women being involved in warfare, or at least associated with weaponry.

The extent to which women were part of the Egyptian military is a subject rarely tackled. It is particularly noticeable that previous works covering Egyptian warfare fail to make any mention of women in a military context. Nevertheless, together with the position of women within Egyptian society as a whole, the roles of New Kingdom female monarchs such as Ahhotep, Hatshepsut, Nefertiti, and Tawosret need to be scrutinized far more closely. This is especially the case given the apparent warrior-like sensibilities of earlier women rulers such as Nitocris of the Old Kingdom. If such women could hold positions of political power, it is a possibility that some may also have held positions of military power. It is not a coincidence that one of the most important deities in ancient Egyptian religion, Sekhmet, the goddess of warfare, was female, while some of the highest offices of state normally held by men could also be held by women. I will be looking more closely at these examples of ancient Egyptian women involved in warfare in Chapter 4.

In a book about warfare and weapons in ancient Egypt, it is important to start off on the right foot. Therefore the first thing I will be looking at is the ancient Egyptian military, before moving on to the typology and development of the weaponry used throughout Predynastic and Dynastic Egypt, with some forays into the Late Period and the Graeco-Roman era as well.

This chapter examines the social context of warfare in Egypt; the reasons for conflict in the 2nd Dynasty, for example, were different to those in the late Eighteenth Dynasty, when the Egyptians were fighting to maintain their empire. I will be looking at the development of the ancient Egyptian offensive military tactics and weaponry as a whole (defensive aspects will be examined in the next chapter) rather than at individual battles (such as the Battle of Kadesh) as numerous works have already examined such battles in great detail.[1] This chapter will also look at certain types of weapons used in ancient Egyptian warfare, including how they developed throughout the Dynastic period, along with specific examples.

Curto[2] provides four specific reasons as to why the Egyptians went to war:

- wars of unification, creating a political and state unity;
- wars of liberation from domination by foreign entities;
- wars of colonial intentions aimed at securing territories;
- imperialistic wars against neighbouring states and in defence of Egypt's boundaries and borders.

This somewhat simplistic view ignores other aspects of warfare that are not an ideology but a practice. Examples of these could be slavery, looting missions, civil war, or assimilations. Curto seems largely concerned with examining artistic depictions of the military rather than the detailed and complex reasons behind why the ancient Egyptians actually went to war (in all of its varying forms). Therefore, his brief and simple explanations really only suffice for those wishing to solely concentrate on artistic aspects of the military. These four examples, however, do describe some of the political influences on Egyptian warfare and it might be possible that similar political influences could be applied to the study of those women known to have been involved in such warfare.

Fighting networks were closely linked to identity within ancient Egyptian society. For example, there was a certain level of prestige attached to membership of a chariot squadron and the ancient Egyptian archer battalions were said to be highly feared, mainly due to the powerful composite bows they used.[3] Part of this chapter will examine the different types of soldier that were found in the ancient Egyptian military, along with their roles within the ancient Egyptian army and any military campaigns that were carried out.

Upholding *ma'at* (the ancient Egyptian concept of truth, justice, balance, and order) was a major responsibility of the Pharaohs of ancient Egypt.[4] This responsibility apparently included the protection of the ancient Egyptian state from foreign invasion, along with preventing foreign powers from interfering in Egypt's territories (agreeing with the four main explanations for ancient Egyptian warfare mentioned above).[5] The New Kingdom apparently ushered in a great deal of this sort of military activity, with contemporary literature providing evidence for the ancient Egyptian's hatred of their foreign neighbours, correlating again with some of the four reasons suggested above.[6]

Looking at the recurrent smiting motif (which is at times evocatively described as head-smashing), these scenes are the longest-standing form of the portrayal of Egyptian enemies.[7] Such smiting scenes are enduring statements of a pharaoh's conquest, rule, and power,[8] with the Sphinx Stela of Amenhotep II clearly describing the way in which the king smashes his mace upon the heads of his enemies (the people of the Nine Bows)[9] **(Figures 1.1 and 1.2)**. This vivid depiction suggests that

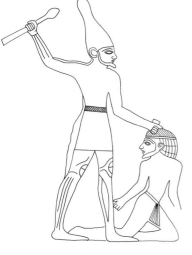

Figure 1.1

the Egyptians believed they would appear powerful as a nation through images of their leader in this particular position of strength. Another such account from the Gebel Barkal stela of Thutmose III details the king as smiting southern enemies and beheading northern enemies,[10] with the accompanying artistic portrayals presumably making the point very clear to a population which was almost entirely illiterate.[11]

Such graphic depictions could also be accompanied by specific phrases, particularly the expression *hr tb(w)t*; apparently translating to 'under the feet', possibly referring to anyone subject to the pharaoh.[12] If an enemy of Egypt was described as being under the sandals, or feet, of the Pharaoh, they were understood to be completely defeated and subjugated by the victorious ruler; a powerful representation of the Egyptians' dominion over their enemies. This phrase is found in varying forms, with Thutmose I on the Tombos Stela claiming that foreign lands were trodden under his feet, whereas his daughter, Hatshepsut, chose to describe all lands as being under her sandals.[13]

This idea of enemies being held under the feet of the pharaoh was frequently used in the Ramesside period and the pharaohs were often shown in artistic portrayals as walking over or treading on their enemies in the heat of battle.[14] This variation, with the enemy under the feet of the pharaoh in active combat, is an even more powerful image which would, presumably, have had the maximum psychological effect on both enemies and the Egyptian populace. This 'enemy under the feet' motif, in whatever form it takes, is related to Curto's third and fourth motives for warfare: colonial intentions.[15] It could be argued that this concept of the 'enemy under the feet' developed into, or might be related to, the modern Middle Eastern gesture of hitting someone with the sole of the shoe to show absolute contempt.

The evidence for the composition and the organisation of the ancient Egyptian army during the Old Kingdom is generally gained

Figure 1.2

from the detailed battle descriptions that are found on the walls of temples, along with lists of titles found on the walls of soldiers' tombs.[16] There is some suggestion, from scholars such as Shaw, that in the early stages of the Old Kingdom, the bureaucracy and the priesthood were far more powerful (and therefore possibly more important) than the military.[17] At this time, the apparent lack of need for a full-time, permanent standing army resulted in there being only a small royal bodyguard in existence, which was supplemented by the conscription of young men.[18] This structuring of the army perhaps reflects the nature of warfare in ancient Egypt during this particular period. The lack of unification, liberation, colonial, or imperial warfare (as set out in Curto 1971) perhaps meant that there was little need for a permanent army and that a conscripted supplement was enough to run the military as required. Indeed, the suggestion is that, for the most part, Dynastic Egypt's soldiers, particularly before the New Kingdom, were not professional troops.[19]

According to scholars such as Shaw and Wilson, army life was apparently not the most attractive of career options for the average ancient Egyptian: a military life takes them away from their beloved homeland and the concept of dying away from Egypt and being buried in a foreign land was one of the worst things an ancient Egyptian could think of.[20] Army life during the early Dynastic period was also very hard, but at least it was in relatively short bursts – there were limitations placed on campaign length in the form of the weather and the harvest season; as many conscripts at this time were taken from the field workers, those men were needed back in the fields in time for both the planting and for the harvest.[21]

This apparent lack of organisation or hierarchy within the Old Kingdom military is accompanied by the only occasional use of the title 'overseer of the soldiers'; there was also the title 'overseer of desert blockhouses and royal fortresses', the possessor of which apparently controlled the fortresses on Egypt's borders.[22] Other than these two overseer titles, the only other military title to appear at this particular time is the word *ṯst*, used to describe units of soldiers during this period and roughly corresponding to the term 'battalion'.[23] However, does this paucity of titles really indicate a lack of military organisation? We cannot be so sure of that. Generally, any time there was a risk to Egypt's borders, an army could be raised explicitly for dealing with the threat and then dismantled almost immediately after the threat had been handled.[24] This suggests a great deal of organisation and infrastructure even if these were temporary, rather than permanent, systems. The size of the army mustered would differ depending upon the circumstances in which it was raised – the troops numbers sent mirrored the size of the threat encountered.[25]

Further evidence for the Old Kingdom military can be seen in the autobiography of Weni, a nobleman from Abydos. Weni describes a campaign in Palestine, during the reign of Pepi I (2332-2283 BC), which led to a large-scale conscription of men from Egypt and Nubia.[26] According to Weni, the army was composed of tens of thousands of soldiers that came from local corps that were provided by provincial officials.[27] This particular campaign also demonstrates Pepi's plans for his nation: the commission made of Weni was to defend only, not to expand Egypt's borders, as Pepi I apparently had no desire to increase the size of his territory.[28] By the time we reach the First Intermediate Period, there had been such devolution of power from central government to the provinces that local governors recruited their own private armies.[29]

As we move onto the Middle Kingdom, we can see that the Egyptian military organisation had become more ambitious and systematic. Shaw argues that this is displayed by Amenemhat I's Nubian policy, as continued by his successors, where the royal army campaigns into the region were initially supported by provincial governors' troops, perhaps the same provincial governors who were supported by private armies during the First Intermediate Period.[30] By the reign of Senwosret III (also known as Senusret or Sesostris), the fifth pharaoh of the Twelfth Dynasty, the governors' power had been greatly reduced; this reduction in power is perhaps due to the existence of a more professional and organised royal army in Nubia.[31] Nubia was certainly important in the development of the ancient Egyptian army, particularly during this period. The need to control Nubia led to the establishment of a whole line of fortresses across boundaries, which then inevitably required permanent garrisons of soldiers.[32]

These Nubian garrisons required a complex network of command, which would necessarily increase the organisation of the ancient Egyptian military. This organisational development is evidenced by a cache of papyri discovered at the later Theban mortuary temple of Ramesses II by James Quibell; this cache included the 'Semna Dispatches', hieratic communiqués between Nubian forts sent during the reign of Amenemhat III.[33] One of the letters deals with the military surveillance of the regions around the Nubian forts and demonstrates two elements of military organisation during the Middle Kingdom. It describes the precise attention to detail from Egyptian bureaucracy to the army and the presence of an intricate chain of command through the ranks.[34]

During the Middle Kingdom, it has been argued by scholars such as Darnell and Manassa that the military titles for infantry companies seemed to refer to the troops of a city, naming the city itself at times, with the forces being made up from several local garrisons.[35] By the time of the New Kingdom, whilst there were still local garrisons, the company names tended not to have local identities and instead the titles came from either the place they were stationed or from the god or goddess with whose temple community the forces were associated.[36] It has been suggested that the regional loyalties in the First Intermediate Period (and the Middle Kingdom) gave way to a more nationally-based military by the early New Kingdom.[37] This perhaps originated in the need for Egypt to unite as a nation to dispel the Hyksos (who had infiltrated from Western Asia), which also resulted in more overt expressions of patriotic feelings. It is clear that the organisation of the ancient Egyptian military differed between the earlier periods (the First Intermediate Period and the Middle Kingdom) and the later period (the New Kingdom).

In the New Kingdom, particularly by the time of the Eighteenth Dynasty (when Egypt had imperialistic concerns), there was the establishment of a large and professional army with an organised hierarchy. This hierarchy seemingly created alternative routes to power which were even open to uneducated men.[38] This meant that the traditional clerical administrators, trained by scribes, had to share military power with a new military class and this new development supposedly played an important role in the rise of the so-called 'warrior pharaohs' who emerged during the Eighteenth to Twentieth Dynasties.[39]

According to Redford, the New Kingdom army comprised of a core of full-time soldiers (who in times of peace would be stationed at the various garrisons throughout Egypt), supplemented during times of war by conscripted men from temple communities.[40] The archery units were apparently the group feared most, mainly due to their use of the composite bow; a weapon that was more powerful by far than its predecessor, the simple bow.[41] These archery units either made up an entire battalion of their own or were attached to various infantry units.[42]

Recruitment into the Egyptian military for the core soldiers, in the New Kingdom at least, began early in a boy's life and boys coming from military families would generally tend to serve in the same units as their fathers.[43] The techniques that the young recruits would learn were part of a rigorous training course: marching techniques, proficiency with weapons, and military discipline were the order of the day for these young soldiers.[44] Some of the New Kingdom literary texts seemed to be designed to discourage young men from joining the army. Papyrus Anastasi III, for example, suggested that for young recruits the training was brutal, with talk of body blows and heads splitting open from the beatings meted out to new recruits within the infantry.[45]

Yet in contrast to the somewhat cynical view of army life presented by Papyrus Anastasi III, other evidence suggests that military life, at least in the New Kingdom, could be fairly agreeable. For example, Ramesses II's Battle of Kadesh reliefs at the temples of Luxor and Abu Simbel portray army life, including the setting-up of a temporary camp. The encamped soldiers are surrounded by a barrier comprised of the soldiers' shields, along with stabling for horses and cattle.[46] The scene is complete with the depiction right in the centre of the encampment of the royal pavilion and the tents of the military hierarchy.[47] Whether or not this is a realistic portrayal, it is certainly a vivid one. It does not, however, illustrate the training of the recruits. Another such example is found in the Memphite tomb of Horemheb and depicts a military camp at rest. Earlier in the Eighteenth Dynasty, Akhenaten's training of young soldiers is described in one of the hymns in a tomb at Amarna, where Akhenaten is credited with training thousands of troops himself.[48]

Whilst the training during the New Kingdom, and indeed during any period of Dynastic Egypt, could be brutal (resulting in a great deal of physical pain and hardship) there were also great rewards to be had from a life in the military. During service, much like the rewards possible from service in the Roman army, there was the possibility of advancement through the army ranks and the ever-present chance of spoils of war from combat victories.[49] Those soldiers who survived the military and active service through to their retirement were gifted with land and livestock. This can be seen in the Wilbour Papyrus, dated to the reign of Ramesses V, which includes veteran soldiers (including Sherden mercenaries) in the lists the people renting land in Middle Egypt.[50] The New Kingdom army was also supported by a small army in itself of craftsmen (necessary for creating and maintaining the weaponry), porters, drivers, animal handlers, and cooks, to name but a few (much as with any army, ancient or modern).[51]

During the New Kingdom an edict issued by Horemheb states that, within the country of Egypt itself, there were two army corps which corresponded to the north and south of the country (Lower and Upper Egypt respectively).[52] The royal bodyguard positions were served in ten-day cycles, with provincial soldiers serving the shifts. In contrast, during a campaign, there were three or four principal divisions of around 5000 soldiers, made up of a combination of conscripted men and professional full-time soldiers.[53] These divisions took their names from a deity and followed it with a suitable epithet; it is likely that the deity names for the divisions were taken from the local deity of the area from which the soldiers had been recruited.[54]

The ancient Egyptian infantry had a hierarchical structure that resembled the armies of most developing civilisations, including the highest rank in the Middle Kingdom (the 'great overseer of the army') which could be said to be the equivalent of the Western rank of general.[55] The title of 'general' (not actually an ancient Egyptian term but a modern English translation) itself appears rarely until the reign of Amenhotep III. It is at this point that there was a major reorganisation of the Egyptian military and a more comprehensive division of the infantry and the chariotry.[56] As stated above, there was a core group of full-time soldiers supplemented by conscripted men in times of war,[57] with some later Eighteenth Dynasty soldiers spending their whole working lives in the army.[58] However, it was more common for careers to combine both military administrative service and work in civil administration.[59]

The infantry was generally divided into units known as companies, which comprised several groups of fifty men that were then divided further still into platoons of ten.[60] Companies could comprise different armaments; some were made up only of archers whereas others were infantry armed with weapons such as spears and axes designed primarily for close-combat situations. These companies would take their names from their pharaoh, sometimes referring to the monarch's battle-prowess.[61] This changed during the reign of Akhenaten, with associations with the Aten (as well as their pharaoh) being included.[62]

The extent of the military innovations achieved by the ancient Egyptians is open to debate. The development of armour will be discussed in more detail in Chapter 3. Briefly, however, armour development was seemingly restricted to padded caps and rawhide shields, with the chariots apparently designed for speed rather than protection and force.[63] The chariot driver did wear a level of protective clothing, including some body armour and a helmet of either leather or bronze, while the other chariot passenger would be armed with a bow and javelins.[64] This armour and chariot design would suggest that the Egyptian soldiers were perhaps not strong in defence and relied mainly on their weapons and mode of attack. This suggestion is conjecture on the part of Redford based on the lack of armour development in Egypt.[65]

The chariot was used by the *maryannu*, who were an elite corps within the New Kingdom army,[66] and have been described as young heroes; part of an aristocratic warrior class modelled on an Asiatic military elite also named *maryannu*.[67] The *maryannu* are referred to variously as chariot warriors[68] and also as army aristocracy.[69] The general consensus is that the *maryannu* were elite soldiers and charioteers and, for some, the *maryannu* were the most ostentatious chariot warriors of the ancient world.[70] The chariotry was organised into groups of fifty and had a very important administrative infrastructure; during, and after, the Eighteenth Dynasty, the administrative titles were not limited to non-combatants alone; chariot warriors could also hold these titles.[71]

By the time of the New Kingdom, warfare between Egypt and enemies from the Near East became a battle between the elite units, with a definite emphasis on the chariotry.[72] Being part of a chariot unit required not only a great deal of wealth but great skill and specialisation; the skills needed to control a chariot moving at speed, as well as firing arrows when travelling at such speeds, requiring considerable practice, enhancing the status of those who were involved in the chariotry.[73] The two soldiers associated with the chariot are generally described as 1) the warrior and 2) the driver and shield-bearer.[74]

The bow and arrow has been described as the weapon of choice for the *maryannu*;[75] they were apparently devoted to sports such as shooting with the bow and arrow, javelin-throwing, and the art of fighting from chariots.[76] The construction of the chariot itself, and the form its crew took, ensured the creation of an effective fast-moving stage from which weapons such as the bow and arrow and the javelin could be effectively utilised.[77] The power of the composite bow meant that it was used a great deal in chariot-fighting and it was appreciably shorter than a self-bow making it more manageable in a chariot.[78] With expertise such as this it is not surprising that the *maryannu* were seen as elite soldiers.

The Egyptian army at times also had troops known as 'auxiliaries'; foreign troops that would serve in each branch of the ancient Egyptian military, either integrated into existing units or in their own separate units.[79] These foreign troops would use specific weapons that differed from those used by the native Egyptian troops, as well as carrying out tasks that were particular to them and their skills.[80] As with the Roman Army, comprised of soldiers from many different countries and states in the Roman Empire, some auxiliaries seemingly became members of Egyptian society, having served in the Egyptian military for a sufficient length of time. Acculturation, such as instruction in the Egyptian language, and rewards, such as the provision of land upon retirement, would be used at times by the Egyptians to ensure the loyalty of their foreign troops.[81] This could be an effective technique; if a foreign soldier spent enough time away from his home and acclimatised to his new surroundings, then he might well begin to display some loyalty to his new 'home'. The promise of a worthwhile reward at the end of his service would only increase loyalty to the Egyptian army, since land was a highly valuable commodity. Again, there are obvious parallels here with the design and procedures of the Roman army.

The first recorded auxiliary troops were apparently the Nubians, recruited to fight for the Upper Egyptians during the First Intermediate Period in their campaign against the Heracleopolitans in Lower Egypt.[82] These Nubian recruits, called the Medjoy (or Medjay), were later renowned for their roles in the ancient Egyptian military, as the ancient Egyptian equivalent of policemen, as well as being archers and scouts.[83] The Medjoy continued to be in use in the Middle Kingdom, apparently playing a crucial role in pharaoh Kamose's re-conquest of Egypt towards the end of the Second Intermediate Period, and during the New Kingdom. Indeed, by the time of the Eighteenth Dynasty the term Medjoy no longer referred to just Nubian soldiers but was used in reference to policemen and patrolmen in general.[84] These Nubian troops were very much in demand, with examples of Egyptian vassals in Syria-Palestine requesting the aid of these soldiers in order to successfully defend their cities during the Amarna period.[85]

There were other foreign troops that served in the ancient Egyptian military, with instances of Asiatics serving in the ancient Egyptian army, though (in the Old Kingdom at least) they were rarer than the Nubian auxiliaries.[86] By the Middle Kingdom period, there were times when Asiatic military units were actually settled within Egypt's borders,[87] which again is a practice that has definite parallels with the structure of the Roman army.

It is worth briefly looking at Dynastic Egypt's forays into naval warfare, although the navy (such as it was) was certainly not as extensive as the navies of contemporary nations/states. For much of the Dynastic Period, shipping in the Mediterranean was mostly commercial, not military, but this seemed to change towards the latter part of the New Kingdom, when the Delta coastline was under threat from several sea-borne foreign armies.[88] For example, there was a raid by Sherden pirates in the second year of Ramesses II's reign; these pirates were not only defeated, but were also incorporated into the Egyptian military as mercenaries.[89] However, Ramesses II's reaction to this seemed to be the building of multiple fortresses along the coastline, rather than increasing the number of military ships.[90]

Most of the time, the ancient Egyptian fleet seems to have been used more for the transport of troops to battlefields as quickly as possible for the active engagement in naval battles.[91] For example, towards the end of the Second Intermediate Period, Kamose (making a point to emphasise the amount of timber to be used in the construction of the flotilla) arranged for his fleet to lay siege to the Hyksos capital of Avaris, the soldiers and war supplies being transported to the site more quickly than they could be by marching overland.[92] This would change to some extent later in the New Kingdom, but not hugely.

Much of the evidence for actual naval battles and warships seem to come from the reign of Ramesses III, when (in the eighth year of his reign) the Sea Peoples attacked at the Delta border. They came first over land (but were defeated in a single battle at the northern edge of the Sinai desert) and then by sea, where they were defeated in what seems to have been a fairly epic naval battle.[93] This naval battle is portrayed at the mortuary temple of Medinet Habu, where the relief depicts hand-to-hand combat between the Sea Peoples (on five boats) and the Egyptians (on four boats which were, naturally, larger than their Sea Peoples counterparts).[94] Ancient Egyptian artistic sensibilities and aesthetics must be taken into account here and it is safe to say that perhaps the numbers of vessels depicted on the reliefs do not accurately reflect the actual numbers that took part in the battle.[95] It is possible, as with the smiting scenes discussed elsewhere, the artists were instructed to portray the superiority of the Egyptian fleet, or maybe there simply was not enough room on the relief to fit in the correct numbers of vessels.

The Egyptian vessels have rows of up to twenty-two oarsmen along with archers and foot-soldiers (although the exact numbers are difficult to discern with any precision), outnumbering the people on board the Sea Peoples vessels, where it is argued that the figures on-board must have doubled-up as warriors and rowers.[96] The Egyptian vessels are described as having low prows, high, angular sterns, with 'aftercastles' of two storeys, and a high bulwark.[97] The Sea Peoples boats were angular, with vertical prows and sterns (very much in the tradition of Aegean ships), designed to do well on long sea voyages.[98] One of the Sea Peoples vessels has seemingly capsized or been brought down by the Egyptian flotilla and the Sea Peoples dead are seen floating in the surrounding water.[99] As with the Sherden pirates discussed above, the Sea Peoples were apparently also assimilated into ancient Egyptian empire after Ramesses III's victory, although in the long-term this solitary victory was only putting-off the unavoidable as the region of Canaan was lost to the Sea Peoples by the end of the Twentieth Dynasty.[100]

It would seem that most of the time, particularly during the latter part of the Dynastic Period, any Egyptian fleet was mostly used to protect and enforce Egypt's trade interests. For example in the Twenty-Sixth Dynasty, the Saite pharaohs created a large fleet of war-galleys, in the style of Graeco-Phoenician ships, in order to regain (albeit temporarily) control of trade in the Levantine.[101]

Despite this evidence for some aspect of naval warfare later on in Dynastic Egypt, throughout most of the Dynastic Period Egypt's military forces were chiefly land-based, resorting to naval battles rarely, with the flotilla mostly being used to transport equipment and soldiers to battles.[102] Certainly, there is a dearth of evidence for Egypt's flotilla in the New Kingdom, but there is a wealth of evidence for the land-based forces; this either suggests that the sea-based military was not as important or developed as the land-based army, or that there is simply an annoying lack of primary resources providing relevant information.[103] The former is the most likely explanation, with the land-based military indeed being far more advanced and essential to Dynastic warfare than the ancient Egyptian navy (such as it was).[104]

2

Weapons in Ancient Egypt

Of the numerous types of weaponry employed in Dynastic Egypt, considerable amounts of research have been carried out in connection with each and every one of them. This section is where the real fun begins, looking at some of the most common weapon types that were present throughout Dynastic Egyptian history.

Axe (Figures 2.1 and 2.2)

The axe was a weapon of some importance in ancient Egypt, being seen in a wide range of forms and variations from Predynastic Egypt all the way through to the Graeco-Roman period. The Egyptian deity Anat, introduced into Egypt from Syria-

Figure 2.1

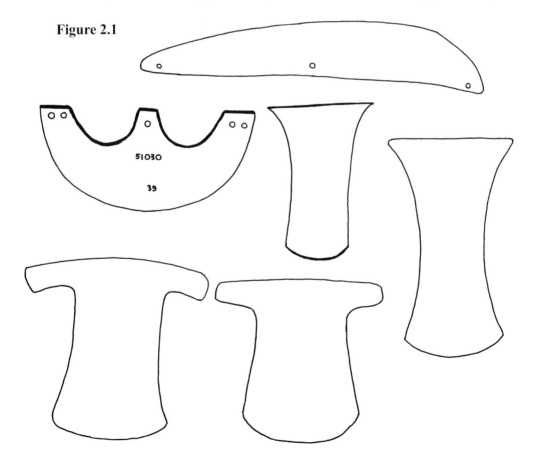

Palestine, first appeared in the late Middle Kingdom and was primarily a goddess of warfare, often depicted with a shield, an axe, and a lance.[105] The axe was seen as symbolically important, at least in the late Middle Kingdom period and very possibly into the New Kingdom and Late Period. Axes, along with maces and spears, were the close-combat weapons of choice for the Egyptian infantry right up until the New Kingdom when swords began to be more widely used.[106]

The axe was present as an artefact and in art throughout the Dynastic Period, with early examples dating to the Predynastic period and the Old Kingdom; though it can be difficult to distinguish axes used in battle from the non-combat tools of the period.[107] By the late Predynastic period there was already a highly developed knowledge of copper-smelting and large axe-heads were being produced.[108] Axes were represented in the Old Kingdom tomb of Khamehesit at Saqqara, where they were depicted with crescent blades and curved hafts, tucked into the kilts of soldiers on siege ladders.[109] Socket axes were seemingly manufactured in the Old Kingdom, although no remains of these particular axes have been found from this time.[110] Dating from the reign of Djet, several burials discovered in the Memphite cemeteries contained copper axes; these axes were inscribed with the Horus name of Djet below a boat borne on wings in which a falcon rides.[111]

One of the most detailed sources for ancient Egyptian axes is the work of Vivian Davies, whose catalogue held in the British Museum is the most comprehensive source for the many different types found to date.[112] Davies provides several examples of early Dynastic and Old Kingdom axes, the main materials for which would appear to be either copper or arsenical copper. For example, a Late Predynastic or

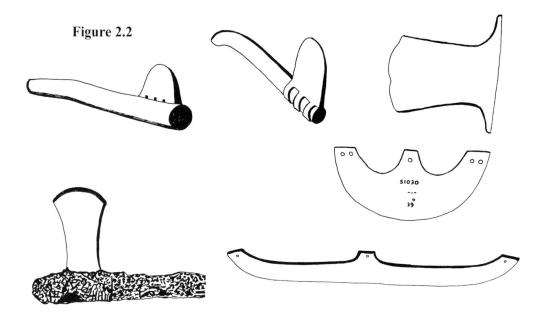

Figure 2.2

early First Dynasty axe [51185] from an A-Group cemetery in Faras was composed of arsenical copper. The axe-head was rectangular in shape, had a narrow, elongated blade, along with slightly convex sides and butt. According to Davies the edge of the axe-head had been hammered more from one side than it had been from the other. Analysis of the axe-head revealed that the composition was over 98% copper and a small amount of arsenic, with trace amounts of other metals.[113] This small amount of arsenic would have strengthened the blade somewhat, as copper alone is not a particularly strong metal. It would seem that the addition of arsenic was an early method for deliberately strengthening the metal, creating a more effective and longer-lasting weapon.

There are, however, plenty of examples of axe-heads composed almost entirely of pure copper, with only the smallest trace amounts of other metals in evidence. A First Dynasty example [30065], possibly from Amelineau's excavations at Abydos (1895-1898), is made of over 99% copper. It is another rectangular axe-head, with a concave butt and convex sides, one of which is shorter and more convex than the other, giving the cutting edge a somewhat lopsided appearance. This cutting edge displays some signs of wear, suggesting that perhaps this axe was used in conflict. There are also markings on one face which are similar to the hieroglyphs and which may possibly represent the personal name of the axe's owner.[114]

Other Old Kingdom axes had slightly more complex forms as the axe technology developed through the Dynasties. From the late Second Dynasty onwards, in the British Museum collection at least, single-hole form axes were being made.[115] These axes would have a single binding-hole, often cast into the blade during its manufacture, so that it could be more easily affixed to the haft. Even well into the Old Kingdom stone was still occasionally used to make axes; stone such as flint and chert was often used and it is not uncommon to find stone axe-heads with edges that still retain some level of sharpness.[116]

Bronze axe-heads seemingly first made an appearance in the First Intermediate Period. Certainly, the first appearance of a bronze axe-head in Davies' catalogue is a lugged, perforated, round form axe-head [68873], cautiously dated First Intermediate Period to Middle Kingdom, with no recorded provenance. Though this is one of the first occurrences of a bronze axe-head in Davies' catalogue, it is unlikely to be the first occurrence of a bronze axe-head in Egyptian history. This axe-head is thickly corroded and the cutting edge appears to have sustained damage due to use. What is interesting about this particular axe-head is that traces of the original wooden haft survive along the butt, as well as the remains of the original binding in one of the lateral holes.[117]

During this period, copper seems to have remained one of the most popular materials for casting axe-heads, a preference that appears to have continued into the Middle Kingdom. For example, a rounded axe-head dated to the Middle

Kingdom [30083] was made of arsenical copper and still had the original wooden haft and metal fastening in place.[118] One 'edged-baton' axe-head [51038], dated by Davies from the First Intermediate Period to the early Middle Kingdom, is made of arsenical copper. The axe-head is shallow and symmetrical, with a wide, convex cutting edge, a concave butt, and short lugs that appear slightly hooked.[119] The fact that other similar axe-head examples, from around the same period, are composed of arsenical copper as well suggests that bronze was not yet the popular option for casting axes that it would later become.

This same period also saw some axe-heads that were made of bronze but it was from the Middle Kingdom, and well into the Second Intermediate Period, that bronze became the metal of choice for casting axes. By the Middle Kingdom, McDermott mentions that there were occurrences of votive and functional axes being placed in the burials of men, women and children.[120] Often interred as individual objects, axes could also be included in weapon groups and were used as amulets; miniature hatchets sometimes being worn around the neck.[121] As well as being composed of stone, Middle Kingdom axes could also have been made of bronze and copper and some precious metals, such as silver, were used when decorating some ceremonial weapons.[122] The materials used on the haft of the axes varied from linen to plant material which may have been in place to ensure that there was an efficient grip for the soldier wielding the axe. As well as the haft covering, the haft was also usually curved allowing for an expert swing and the prevention of slippage during use. In addition to this, during the Middle Kingdom, some axe handles had straps attached to them, perhaps allowing for them to be tied onto the body whilst being carried outside of combat.[123]

The physical appearance of the axe as a weapon changed somewhat over time, with several different varieties being manufactured in the Middle Kingdom. The traditional battle-axe of the Middle Kingdom was the tanged (small projections), crescentic hatchet.[124] There were three dominant styles of this hatchet axe, although all of these axe types were designed with shallow and wide-cutting edges). The first, and most common, type was a hatchet blade that had three perforations. The second style has similarities with the first one described, but has hooked lugs and the seemingly traditional Middle Kingdom crescent-shaped blade that is segmented. The third type of this hatchet axe was designed to be a slashing axe with blades that could be symmetrical and asymmetrical.[125] There was another variation of Middle Kingdom axe, one which was designed with tangs, usually three of them, with each tang being perforated with one or more holes (which enabled this type of axe-head to be fastened to the haft using either cord or small nails).[126] It would seem that this tanged, flat cutting axe was a style that was limited to Egypt during the Middle Kingdom.[127]

Based on the composition of the copper alloys, Davies arrived at the conclusion that specific types of axe were designed for military purposes.[128] Davies noticed that the battle-axe blades contained high percentages of tin-bronze and arsenic, whereas the blades of tools of this type had relatively low percentages of arsenic-copper, ensuring that the battle-axes were fairly lightweight.[129] The slashing axe was dated, by Davies, to the First Intermediate Period or the early Middle Kingdom.[130] During the Middle Kingdom 'duck-bill' axes were also relatively common, remaining in use during the Second Intermediate Period even when more rounded axe forms were developed.[131]

It is likely that there were some outside influences on the axe during the Middle Kingdom. Asiatic, or eye, fenestrated axes were supposedly brought into Egypt by foreign couriers, although they did not seem to be adopted by the Egyptian army on any large scale.[132] Indeed, the tanged cutting axe was much preferred by the Egyptians than the socketed axe that was a favourite in western Asia; the socketed axe depended on their sharp blades for cutting into unprotected flesh.[133]

It is possible that the different axe types had varied uses outside of active warfare. For example, the weapons could be used to denote rank and status. There is also the theory that soldiers protecting river vessels were armed with hatchets whereas soldiers hired to accompany and protect hunting parties were armed with axes.[134]

During the upheaval of the Second Intermediate Period, when Egypt was controlled by the Hyksos, artistic representations of soldiers and their weaponry are few and far between.[135] However, remains examined by Davies indicated that the axes in this period were generally lugged with either splayed blades or curved sides.[136] One example, a battle-axe with a wooden handle and the cartouche of a King named Nebmaatra engraved on the blade, was found in a pan grave at Mostagedda that was dated to the Second Intermediate Period.[137]

The overthrow of the Hyksos led to the formation of the New Kingdom period, the first dynasty of which was the Eighteenth Dynasty. The design and use of the axe as a weapon went through significant changes during the New Kingdom. During this time there were examples of hatchets and model/votive axes that were found in foundation and funerary deposits, including small toy-like axes amongst goods in child burials.[138] According to scholars such as McDermott, with regard to the more functional axes of the period, it would seem that new axes were starting to be designed in response to the recent developments in the armour of the enemies; these new designs had shorter lugs and narrower blades, seemingly replacing the epsilon axe that was so popular during the Old and Middle Kingdoms, first appearing in excavated remains at Deir el-Ballas.[139]

The beginning of the Eighteenth Dynasty also saw the manufacture of symmetrical axes which had elongated lugs, with bronze pins securing the blade while hide thongs bound the handle in order to prevent the wood from splitting;[140] though this could also possibly have been a method of increasing the grip of the person using the weapon, along with protecting the wood. Later in the same dynasty, the major battle-axe was the asymmetrical axe, the narrow axe-head designed to pierce scale-armour as well as skin, the blade being held in the wound upon impact. Earlier axe-heads had a wider cutting edge and were very effective against exposed and lightly clothed skin, but would have been less so against armour.[141] The 'duck-bill' axe (mentioned above) was the style that was replaced in the New Kingdom by this splayed-type axe-head with straight sides; the latter's penetration capability is most likely responsible for the change in styles, due to the development of body armour in the New Kingdom period.[142]

In the later New Kingdom, it would seem that some axe-heads were cast in two-piece closed moulds and were then hafted onto the shaft of the axe; these New Kingdom axes were generally less ornamental than the axes used in earlier periods.[143] There were, however, examples of axes with engravings, such as royal cartouches or other identification marks, engraved on the axe-blade or on the shaft of the base.[144] As many axes during this period were clearly pierced it would seem that there was a strap attached to the handle, securing the axe to the shoulder; a practice that was likely only used in the New Kingdom.[145] While the axe remained an important weapon throughout the Eighteenth Dynasty, it at times appeared to be gradually replaced with the sickle sword (the *khopesh*).[146] By the New Kingdom, an axe was introduced which was often displayed in the possession of royalty: the cast socket hatchet. These axes, foreign in origin, were found at various New Kingdom sites and were cast in a two-piece closed mould. It would appear that double-headed axes were used very rarely by ancient Egyptian soldiers.[147]

By the time of the New Kingdom, bronze became the main metal of choice, with some examples being found at New Kingdom sites such as Amarna.[148] Despite this, simple copper was still in occasional use; one such example was an Eighteenth Dynasty axe-head found in the foundation deposit of the temple of Osiris at Abydos.[149] This axe-head is not made from arsenical copper but just over 99% copper, with only the smallest trace amounts of lead, tin and arsenic. However, there is good reason for this; this particular axe-head is one of a group of seven objects that were found in the foundation deposits, all of which were models.[150] It is not imprudent to assume that during this period, copper was used primarily for model weapons, rather than wasting bronze on their manufacture.

Although bronze was no doubt the metal of choice, there was some evidence of iron being used to manufacture axe-heads during the later stages of the New Kingdom. One Twentieth Dynasty example discussed by Davies, found at Abydos [67587], has been identified as being composed of iron, although the level of corrosion has prevented detailed metallographic analysis; a portion of the blade is missing and the surface bears several deep cracks.[151] As it is made of iron, the axe-head weighs well over 350 g and is much heavier than other examples; this would have made it a formidable weapon if wielded in active combat.[152]

Even in these later periods (c.1549BC – 945BC) iron weapons were relatively rare, although there was an example of an iron halberd found at a Twentieth Dynasty site in Abydos, which is thought to be an early example of an iron weapon (although an iron dagger found in Tutankhamun's tomb is earlier).[153] There were some examples of iron axes found at Soleb, in the Meroitic cemetery, along with a very similar axe discovered in a disturbed site at the Ramesseum, and model axes found at Deir el-Bahri were made of iron, all of which had hooked lugs.[154] The use of iron in ancient Egypt began later than in other early societies (with Shaw and Boatright highlighting ancient Anatolia as one of the first places where iron production occurred) but iron was increasingly used in the later periods, from the later New Kingdom onwards.[155]

Generally speaking, bronze seems to have remained the most popular choice for the manufacture of axe-heads, even into the Third Intermediate and Ptolemaic periods. There were still occasional examples of iron and copper being used, although these appear to have been few and far between. In Davies' catalogue, there is one example of an iron axe-head that is dated to the Graeco-Roman Period; this axe-head [36288] has not succumbed to the same degree of heavy corrosion generally seen in other examples of iron axes, although the corrosion levels are still quite high.[156] Half the cutting edge of the blade is also missing and the other half is cracked and damaged through wear and use, although what remains of the edge is apparently very sharp.[157] This damage, severe though it seems, has not prevented metallographic analysis from being carried out, unlike with some of the examples of iron axes above. The analysis shows that the axe-head is composed of almost 100% iron, with trace samples of nickel and cobalt; the weight of this iron axe-head is impressive, being measured at well over 500 g; another potentially formidable weapon.[158]

Figure 2.3

Some believe that artistic depictions of the axe in ancient Egyptian art are accurate in their execution because of the large quantity of comparable axe remains.[159] Yet in terms of how the axe was utilised, this may not necessarily be the case, given the conventions and restrictions inherent within Egyptian art. The standard one-handed striking or smiting stance taken by armed figures portrayed, which lasted throughout the entire Dynastic and post-Dynastic period relatively unchanged, is not a pose that the human body is able to comfortably maintain (**Figure 2.3**). Therefore, it should not necessarily be assumed that the axe as a weapon would have been wielded exactly in the manner depicted on tomb or temple scenes. There will likely have been distinct similarities but the depictions will have been severely limited by the artistic styles and conventions of the period.

In the Middle Kingdom, tanged axes depicted in hieroglyphic texts were common, as were depictions of soldiers bearing axes.[160] During the Eighteenth Dynasty, a scene from the side of the king's chariot from the tomb of Thutmose IV (in the Valley of the Kings) shows the pharaoh advancing from the right side, preparing to smite the Asiatic foes with a battle-axe held in his right hand. This reflects the stereotypical pose held in the smiting scene throughout Dynastic Egypt.[161] Another Eighteenth Dynasty wall scene fragment, from a temple of Thutmose II at Thebes, depicts Thutmose II in battle. At least one of the Asiatic enemies is carrying a duck-billed axe, a weapon that (according to Spalinger) was more typical to the Middle Kingdom, and by the New Kingdom Period had mostly been replaced by more sophisticated axe types.[162] Spalinger's explanation is that the Palestinians were perhaps not as technologically advanced as the Syrians, Babylonians, or Egyptians;[163] although this could also be a matter of artistic propaganda from the Egyptians, displaying their apparent superiority and technological sophistication over their enemies.

In relation to the Nineteenth and Twentieth Dynasties, it seems that there has been an increased reliance on artistic representations of axes as the physical evidence is somewhat lacking; at this time we see representations of thick- and wide-bladed axes in siege scenes, wielded by sappers. Soldiers were also portrayed in ceremonial and martial situations, pressing the axe flat against the breast to salute a superior.[164] In the Nineteenth Dynasty, the axe developed elongated lugs, producing thick and heavy axes, although few soldiers bore axes of this type in Ramesses II's army.[165]

Whilst depictions of the axe in ancient Egyptian art appear to be mainly related to men, the axes that have been discovered in female burials (the most famous of which is that of Ahhotep) show that the axe was a weapon which could also be associated with women. Yet little work has been done on this specific subject and there remains a tendency to suggest that such weapons found in female burials were merely votive objects (something that will be discussed in Chapter 4). Outside of issues of gender and gender roles within ancient Egyptian warfare though, the axe was obviously a weapon of some importance in ancient Egyptian history, all the way through from the Predynastic period to the New Kingdom and the Late Period. Not only was the axe important as a functional weapon of warfare but it also had symbolic meaning on some occasions.

Bow and Arrow (Figure 2.4).

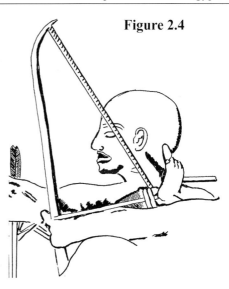

Figure 2.4

The bow and arrow is one of the most recognisable weapons from the history of warfare in general as well as from ancient Egyptian warfare. This basic long-range weapon was in use in ancient Egypt from the outset of the Dynastic period and had also been used in the late Predynastic period.[166] Predynastic tombs have produced evidence of the earliest bows and arrows, the remains of quivers having been excavated from archaic tombs. These quivers were made from several panels of stitched leather and contained differing numbers of arrows, from five up to seventy-nine.[167] In the Predynastic period artistic representations of bows and arrows are relatively uncommon, although the Hunter's Palette does depict the hunter-warrior figures with quivers carried on their backs.[168]

The first bow in use in Dynastic Egypt was the simple, or self, bow, which was fashioned from a stave of almost-straight wood, trimmed at both ends in order to create a tapered effect. The wood needed to be long enough to be bendable without breaking, which may have been achieved through steaming the wood in order to make it more pliable for manufacturing the bow.[169] These impressively simple but effective production techniques used to manufacture the bow changed relatively little throughout the Dynastic period, even as the style of bow altered.[170]

As few as the examples of bows and arrows are in the Predynastic period, they appear to be even fewer in number in the Old Kingdom. Old Kingdom artistic representations and material remains are rare.[171] However, this does not necessarily imply that the bow and arrow was not utilised in the Old Kingdom. Instead, it is more likely that the Old Kingdom evidence simply has not survived as well as evidence from later periods. One example from the Old Kingdom is a dyed leather quiver, whose opening was drawn together by knotted cords still in place.[172]

The simple bow was employed well into the New Kingdom, as shown by the examples from the tomb of Tutankhamun, which still had some animal-gut strings in place when found.[173] Though the simple bow remained in use in the New Kingdom, the composite bow was introduced at the start of this period; this was much stronger than the simple bow and was much more effective as a weapon.[174] One of the major changes which revolutionised and modernised the Egyptian military in the New Kingdom, the composite bow was essentially a wooden core with a layer of sinew applied to the back and a layer of horn applied to the face; this was then enclosed with a protective covering of ash- or birch-bark.[175]

There have been studies that looked at the types of wood employed in the manufacture of bows. One such study examined six bows that were held in the Ashmolean Museum in Oxford and the Phoebe Hearst Museum in Berkeley, California.[176] Three of the bows were dated to the First Intermediate Period, one was dated to the Sixth Dynasty (or possibly First Intermediate Period), and another to the Ninth or Tenth Dynasty; the final bow was undated.[177] The undated bow [1885.375] was from the Ashmolean and was a complete self (or simple) bow found at Thebes; the botanical analysis revealed the bow was most likely made from acacia wood.[178] The Sixth Dynasty bow [6-1588], from the Hearst Museum and found at Naga el-Deir cemetery 3500, was actually a bow fragment. It was the nock end of a self bow which analysis again showed to have been made from acacia.[179] The Ninth or Tenth Dynasty self bow [1921.1301], an Ashmolean artefact, was originally from Sidmant and was practically complete except for one end; the botanical analysis once again revealed this bow to have been manufactured from acacia.[180] Looking at these particular bows, it would appear that acacia was the favoured wood of choice in the Old Kingdom and First Intermediate Period.

The three First Intermediate Period bow fragments were all from the Hearst Museum collection, having been found at the site of Naga el-Deir; although only two of them had cemetery attributions (cemetery 3500).[181] The first of these [6-2757] was the nock-end of a self bow which botanical analysis revealed to be composed of sidder wood. The second bow fragment [6-2778] was also the nock end of a self bow and was composed of tamarisk wood. The final of these three bow fragments (also the nock end of a self bow) had no cemetery or tomb attribution, but was shown to be manufactured from acacia.[182] All of these bows and bow fragments were made from wood sourced from trees indigenous to ancient Egypt,[183] which could mean that the availability of the types of wood took precedence over the precise mechanical properties of the wood.

Prior to the use of swords and spears in the ancient Egyptian military, it is believed that the bow and arrow was the main weapon of choice (for long-range combat at least) and remained a very popular weapon for warfare in general.[184] As the composite bow was introduced the power of the bow as a weapon was increased. By the time of the composite bow, bronze arrowheads on reed shafts were also in use. Due to the strengthened wood of the composite bow, the bowstring was tauter and the arrows could therefore inflict greater damage than when fired from previous simple bows.[185] This is an area where experimental archaeology, demonstrating the effectiveness of such bows and arrows, would provide useful information to compare with wounds found on mummified human remains.

The bows used in ancient Egypt have in fact been the subject of experimental archaeology, when Miller *et al.* carried out a study entitled 'Experimental Approaches to Ancient Near Eastern Archery' which included an examination of ancient Egyptian bows and arrows.[186] The study looked at the reliability, accuracy and power of such weapons by evaluating the comparative performances of a spear, a modern African simple bow, and two replica ancient Egyptian angular composite bows.[187] The weapons were replicated and the velocities of the projectiles appropriate to each type of weapon recorded; the results of this experiment showed a clear linear trend in the improved performance of the weapons.[188] This is the sort of work that could be very successfully extended through comparative studies that look at the impact of such weapons on human tissue (such as comparing the wounds seen on mummified ancient Egyptian remains with the results of testing weapons on human proxies).

As mentioned previously, composite bows could be reinforced with the compressive strength of horn and the tensile strength of sinew.[189] It would seem that, in relation to the composite bow, it was not the thin wooden core that was important for the power of the bow but the horn and sinew. It was vital for the sinew and horn to be precisely aligned in order to allow for the maximum storage and release of energy.[190] The horn and sinew were bonded onto the wooden core, which could be made of non-resinous wood such as poplar or ash.[191]

All of the composite bow examples that have been found in Egypt were discovered in tombs; they do not appear to have been particularly rare or costly, as many of them were found in non-royal tombs.[192] The bows found in tombs were probably a mixture of votive objects (bought specifically for the tomb resident to use in the afterlife) and functional bows (used by the owner in life, before being placed in the tomb with them in death).

So why did the ancient Egyptian bow develop along the lines it did? The appearance of the composite bow, along with the introduction of other military developments such as the chariot, has generally been seen as a result of Egypt's need to keep up with the military advances of neighbouring countries.[193] These developments were often influenced by Egypt's enemies, such as the idea that the chariot came from the Hyksos and the *khopesh* from Canaan (the region that encompasses modern Israel, Lebanon and the Palestinian territories).[194] Egypt's New Kingdom monarchs were particularly concerned with preventing any reoccurrences of the Hyksos infiltration that led to the Second Intermediate Period.[195]

One of the earliest metal arrowheads recovered in Egypt has been dated to the Second Dynasty and was found at Saqqara.[196] In earlier periods arrowheads could be made from flint or wood, with metal arrowheads being developed later;[197] there are examples of Neolithic stone tool assemblages found in Egypt that contained substantial number of projectiles and points.[198] These projectile points were stone arrowheads, displaying evidence of hunting technology for the period.[199] Ebonytipped reed arrowheads were found with the bodies of the Slain Soldiers of Montu-hotep II.[200] Ten of the soldiers had been wounded or killed by such arrows and one arrowhead was even found entwined in the hair of one of the mummified soldiers.[201] Copper arrowheads have also been found that dated to the Eleventh Dynasty. The advantage of copper arrowheads was that copper can be shaped into a solid point that can penetrate through soft tissue, but will bend (not shatter) when it hits bone.[202] This would potentially allow for the reuse of these copper arrowheads, reducing waste and providing a vital resupply of arrowheads in the heat of battle.

There are some excellent examples of Late Period (post-New Kingdom) arrowheads that I have catalogued and which show the development of the arrowhead in ancient Egypt (details of which can be seen in the Appendix of this book). The metal arrowheads in the collections at the Harrogate, provisionally dated to the Saite Period (the Twenth-Sixth Dynasty - 664-525 BC), are crafted from bronze and are therefore less flexible than the copper arrowheads of the Middle and New Kingdoms.

The arrow shaft was usually made of a straight and light material, such as reed (which was plentiful in Egypt) although some wooden examples have also been found.[203] There have also been several examples of arrows with feather fletching, as well as arrows that were made without feathers. Fletching gives an arrow greater stability and accuracy, along with increased force, so in all probability feathers were widely used.[204] While this is a reasonable deduction to have made, it is by no means proven by a great quantity of incontrovertible evidence. It could be that the arrows found without feathers may have been in the process of manufacture. In European medieval practice, as the fletching is easily damaged, it is added last of all, just before the arrows are needed.[205] This could well be the case in the fletching of ancient Egyptian arrows. Whilst the development of the bow and arrow as a physical weapon is interesting, equally fascinating is how the weapon was portrayed in ancient Egyptian art.

There are many depictions of the bow and arrow in Egyptian art throughout the entire Dynastic period. One of the most popular depictions of the pharaoh was to portray him controlling a chariot single-handedly while simultaneously firing arrows, either at his enemies in battle or an enemy fortress, stronghold or city under siege. One such example is Seti I, represented on the exterior north wall of the Hypostyle Court at Karnak, firing arrows at the Hittites whilst driving his own chariot without assistance.[206] The pharaoh in this sort of depiction was shown victorious, with the chariot reins tied behind his back; something that resembles the hunting imagery involving pharaohs in other such wall scenes.[207]

Chariot (Figure 2.5)

The chariot was an extraordinarily crucial development in ancient Egyptian

Figure 2.5

warfare; it can be seen as a weapon of sorts, as well as a method of transport. The chariot only came into extensive use in Egypt at the beginning of the New Kingdom and was part of the military modernisation that took place during that period.[208]

Chariots are said to have been introduced into Egypt from a variety of different sources. There is some suggestion that they were introduced from Western Asia, leading to Egyptian warfare to become more dependent upon the procurement of horses.[209] Horses were introduced into Egypt for pulling chariots in between the end of the Middle Kingdom and the start of the New Kingdom, with the domesticated horse reaching Nubia by the end of the Seventeenth Dynasty.[210] One probable theory is that the idea for the chariot first came from the Hyksos who were described as being masters of the use of horses and chariots. This theory suggests that the chariot was introduced into Egypt during the war of liberation between the Thebans and the Hyksos.[211] This is a theory that the majority of ancient Egyptian scholars have agreed with, although there is some suggestion that the Egyptians were familiar with the chariot before the New Kingdom and that chariots were possibly introduced to Egypt, along with the horse, from the Levant.[212]

The Egyptians probably became familiar with the chariot during the Hyksos occupation of the Second Intermediate Period. They seem to have adapted the chariot design for their own use, equipping it to carry just two men,[213] whereas Hittite chariots carried three men.[214] This made the Egyptian chariots lighter and more suitable for first attack and chase.

The probable Asiatic origin of the chariot in Egypt is revealed by several things, including the different woods used in its construction and by the Canaanite names that were given to the different parts.[215] There are also examples of Asiatics being employed by the Egyptians to drive and maintain chariots, although this does not necessarily demonstrate that the chariot was solely an Asiatic invention.[216]

The chariot was introduced at a time when Egyptian warfare was being completely revolutionised; the introduction of both the chariot and the composite bow was a key step in transforming the way in which the Egyptians fought in battle. Chariotry and foot-soldiers who were archers had increasingly important roles in warfare, archers being particularly essential for the success of the chariotry as this combination was extremely effective.[217] Once the chariot was slow or stationary, the chariot-driver could take up his bow and shoot the enemy, whilst the second man in the chariot could either throw a spear or provide protection for the driver by wielding a shield.[218] The main function of the chariot in Egypt was to provide a mobile firing platform for the archers loosing arrows against infantry (rather than against other chariots), along with the means for transporting military equipment to particular sections of the battlefield.[219]

The advancement of the chariot in Egyptian warfare also brought about innovations in arms and armour, from the aforementioned composite bow to the bronze falchion (another term for a sickle-shaped sword or scimitar, also known as a *khopesh*), the bronze battle-axe, and the light javelin or spear; all of which also led to new methods of warfare.[220] Furthermore, there was the development of what could be described as a military aristocracy associated with the growth of the professional organisation of the chariot squadrons.[221] Indeed, one contemporary source composed by a master scribe describes an aristocratic charioteer as squandering the money (given to him by his wealthy family) on an expensive chariot that is driven too furiously but then abandoned when he reaches some mountains. He is then beaten, presumably for his ridiculous and careless behaviour.[222] Clearly only a certain section of society was eligible to become charioteers in the New Kingdom army. They required sufficient wealth to be able to afford both a chariot and a replacement should that be necessary. As the source seems to suggest, a wealthy family would possibly be willing to sponsor a son in the chariotry.

The introduction of the chariot fostered this new social order within the ancient Egyptian military, one which had its own rules and disciplines distinct from the rest of the army.[223] The prestige of the chariotry is reflected in the status of the men who held positions in the chariot divisions. Yuya, the father of Queen Tiy, was a commander of chariotry for his son-in-law Amenhotep III.[224] The third son of Ramesses II was a charioteer and Ramesses II himself stated that his father had been chief of infantry and chariotry during his lifetime.[225]

The chariot certainly seems to have become a prestigious element of the Egyptian military. It also had a significant role in royal iconography, one example of which is the stele of Amenhotep II, which praises him as a trainer of his own chariot horses. During the reign of Thutmose I, the chariot divisions were elite organised military units within the army.[226] Each chariot division had a commander co-ordinating with the 'Major-General' equivalent of the Egyptian army; each division was also administered by three scribes: one in charge of the soldiers, one in charge of the horses, and the third in charge of the stables.[227] The 'major' would be in charge of a group of fifty chariots, with the larger groups under the control of 'colonels'.[228]

As stated previously, the Egyptians did make certain changes to the design of the chariot. Those built in Egypt had light wheels with spokes and the axle was placed towards the rear of the car. The chariot was also given a wide wheel track, which allowed it to make sharp turns without overturning and the chariot car was completely open at the back, allowing two people to drive side by side in it.[229] These changes ensured that when ranged against enemies, such as the Hittites, the Egyptian chariots had increased agility and therefore something of an advantage against their foes.[230] This advantage was displayed during the Battle of Kadesh, when Ramesses II managed to drive off the Hittite troops until reinforcements arrived, pushing the Hittites back.[231] Indeed, one of the chief functions of the chariot was to break up the enemy formations at the beginning of the battle, which it would be able to do if sufficiently agile.[232] However, the lightness of the alterations in the chariot design that the ancient Egyptians made meant that it would be vulnerable in close combat, which is why it was used in conjunction with ranged archery attacks.[233]

The most intact chariots to have survived from the ancient world are the six found in the tomb of Tutankhamun.[234] These six examples provide a wealth of information about the vehicle, including its manufacturing process.[235] The lower part of the chariot was composed of two wheels with four spokes and an axle set towards the rear of the vehicle, with everything apparently held together with a combination of leather, rawhide, and glue.[236] The leather was used for straps that would help hold the wheel together, whereas the rawhide was applied in order to strengthen joints and wheel hubs. As the climate of ancient Egypt was so hot and dry, the regular use of glue and rawhide was a method of manufacture not always possible in other countries where the climate was not so conducive to such methods.[237]

It could certainly be argued that the ancient Egyptian chariot (because of its speed, lightness, and stability) was the most technologically effective chariot made in ancient history.[238] The chariot was quickly absorbed into new Kingdom royal regalia and it became a representation of Pharaoh's dominance, developing into as powerful a symbol as the mace in that respect.[239] One of the first appearances of the chariot in ancient Egyptian literature was on the stele of Kamose, although this is in reference to the chariots of the Hyksos rather than the Egyptians' own chariots.[240]

As an elite section of the military, the chariot has survived better in the visual record than other aspects of ancient Egyptian warfare.[241] One of the most common depictions of a pharaoh shows the ruler riding in a chariot, either into battle or hunting, controlling the chariot with the reins tied behind his back whilst simultaneously firing a bow or wielding a spear or *khopesh* (a prime example being that of the female charioteer shown above).[242] Similar to the ubiquitous smiting scene, this scene of the pharaoh in the chariot is one which displays his power: not only is the pharaoh in complete control of this dangerous vehicle, he is also able to fight off his enemies with relative ease. This is clearly shown in one of the aforementioned war scenes of Seti I at Karnak, which portrays Seti I in battle against the Libyans.[243] Shown on a much larger scale than his Libyan foes to emphasise his status, Seti is controlling the chariot with reins tied behind his back and is wielding a *khopesh* in one hand, while grasping a composite bow in the other.[244] The scores of dead Libyans being trampled by his chariot horses are testament to Seti's power and skill in battle.

In another part of this scene, Seti I is shown in battle with the Hittites, though in this he is slightly less ambitious; he again controls the chariot with the reins tied behind his back, but in this scene he is only firing arrows into his enemies.[245] Countless Libyan enemies, identified by the feathers in their hair, are struck down with the arrows fired by the king. The point of these scenes was to demonstrate visually the king's might and supremacy, his size in comparison to his enemies meant to illustrate his superiority over them in both status and skill.

The chariot was clearly a vehicle that required some strength, but mainly a great deal of skill from the person controlling it. The great Sphinx stela of Amenhotep II describes the pharaoh as having the ability to drive his chariot whilst simultaneously shooting arrows through targets of Asiatic copper that were at the thickness of one palm.[246] An impressive feat certainly, if it is indeed true. Of course, given the Pharaohs' predilection for exaggeration, there is every possibility this description has been embellished just a tad. This passage nonetheless suggests the skill required to control a chariot successfully. It is likely that the ancient Egyptian chariot was used as either a vehicle of speed or as a shock weapon,[247] unlike the heavier chariot counterparts that were used by the Hittites and Assyrians.

Mace

The mace is a very important weapon in ancient Egyptian history and its overall form appears to have changed relatively little over the course of three thousand plus years. It is believed that the ground and polished stone mace-heads first made their appearances as burial goods in Neolithic graves in the Khartoum region and from then went on to become a very common and important feature of ancient Egyptian culture[248] (**Figures 2.6 and 2.7**).

The mace was a weapon that was associated with Horus' one remaining, healthy eye; Horus being a deity named 'the lord of the mace, who smote his foes'.[249] The mace could also be an important piece of regalia that was at times closely connected with royal authority. There are several variations of mace design, including piriform,

conical, hatchet-shaped, and noduled. These different mace-head shapes presumably caused different forms of trauma to the human body, a possibility discussed in relation to experimental archaeology below. There are several examples of the two main types of mace-head (conical and piriform) held in the Harrogate Museum, including a fascinating one where the manufacturer of the mace-head has seriously miscalculated the

Figure 2.6

placement of the hole for the mace handle, realised once they are halfway through the stone that they are seriously off the mark, and then had to start drilling again from the other end (no doubt filled with frustration at this seemingly basic error).

There is some suggestion that the mace was a clumsy weapon; it could be liable to fracturing upon impact and was possibly used as a subsidiary crushing weapon for finishing off enemy soldiers.[250] In this role, the mace became a representation of

Figure 2.7

Figure 2.8

pharaoh's power and dominance,[251] something that is easily shown by the smiting scenes in which the mace is portrayed as the weapon of choice.

Experimental archaeology carried out at the University of York in 2009 made use of replica mace-heads (which were originally created for a pilot study carried out in 2007 by Professor Joann Fletcher and Dr Stephen Buckley) where they were tested on pig heads and carcasses. In the 2009 experiment, though the conical mace-head chipped slightly upon impact with the pig's head, it did not fracture or shatter the whole way through.[252] In fact, this chip on the edge of the mace-head is consistent with the chipping visible on mace heads in the Harrogate Museum collection, suggesting that perhaps some of the damage observed on the original mace-heads was not depositional or post-depositional, but possibly due to the active use of the mace-head pre-deposition[253] **(Figures 2.8 and 2.9)**.

Initially, in Pre- and Early Dynastic times, the conical mace-head is the most common surviving example before being gradually supplanted by the piriform mace-head.[254] It is not certain as to why this is the case, since a previous study[255] suggested that a conical

Figure 2.9

mace-head would cause a great deal more damage than a piriform one in a smiting situation. In experimental archaeology carried out at the University of York in 2009, a pig head struck with a conical mace-head could be seen both by observation and in X-rays to have sustained more damage than the pig head hit with a piriform mace-head.[256] Each time the same person wielded the mace to ensure that the experiment was a fair test of the mace heads' effectiveness as weapons.[257] This preliminary experiment is the springboard for the further archaeological experiments presented later in this book.

One of the most famous mace-heads in early Dynastic Egyptian history is the Scorpion Mace-head, which was discovered in a temple deposit at the site of Hierakonpolis. This mace-head is dated to approximately the same period as the Narmer Palette (**see Figure 1.1**) and replicates a lot of the symbolism present on the Narmer Palette; in fact, the figure represented on the Scorpion mace-head could well be Narmer.[258] At approximately 25 cm high this mace-head would have been too unwieldy to use in active warfare and it is to be supposed that this was a purely votive weapon, perhaps a ceremonial celebration of King 'Scorpion'.[259] The images on the mace-head depict a pharaoh creating fields and controlling the waters of the Nile; this blends into the metaphorical aspects of a pharaoh's rule – not only is the pharaoh representing the abundance of Egypt's fields here but, as the Nile was so vital in sustaining life in Egypt's virtually rainless environment, any individual seen to be able to control it would have been regarded as very powerful indeed.[260] The figure of the monarch is the largest on the Scorpion mace-head, spanning the entire band from top to bottom[261] in an effective form of propaganda, much like that of the Narmer Palette. This pharaoh must be a monarch of considerable authority; commissioning such a piece would be an excellent visual way to display one's power. It can also be argued that the scorpion motif present on the Scorpion mace-head represents the emerging pharaonic power of the newly-created Dynastic Egyptian state.[262]

Another large and highly-decorated votive mace-head found at Hierakonpolis is known as the Narmer mace-head.[263] Portrayed on this mace-head is a pharaoh who is generally assumed to be Narmer; the pharaoh forms the main focus of the scene, sitting enthroned on a high dais underneath a canopy.[264] The pharaoh is wearing the Red Crown and holding the flail, with his body swathed in a long cloak, and is attended by minor figures of fan-bearers, bodyguards with long quarter-staves, and an official who is variously described as either the vizier or the heir-apparent.[265]

The Narmer mace-head, much like the Scorpion Mace-head, appears to be another form of propaganda in which the pharaoh takes part in what may be the official Appearance of the King of Lower Egypt.[266] Although this festival can be dated back to the First Dynasty from inscriptions on the Palermo Stone, it would seem that Millet believes it could have been carried out at an even earlier date, an example of which could well be depicted on the Narmer Mace-head.[267]

The Scorpion mace-head and the Narmer mace-head were both far too big and heavy to be used in active combat. Instead, they are almost certainly examples of ceremonial votive maces, very similar in style and function to the maces we see in modern day civic ceremonies. A well know example is the mace carried in the State Opening of the Parliament of the United Kingdom (where it represents the authority of the monarch) and the maces often seen at university graduation ceremonies. Interestingly, it would certainly seem that the purpose of the ceremonial mace (to represent a sovereign power) has not changed much in the course of the last few thousand years.

The importance of the mace as both a votive and functional weapon is also displayed by its predominance in the numerous smiting scenes that appear throughout dynastic Egyptian history. One of the first such scenes is found on the Narmer Palette, a vitally important object dating to the very beginning of dynastic rule in Egypt. The particular style of the depiction of a smiting scene continues with very little alteration or variation through to the era of Roman rule in Egypt, over three and a half millennia later. The palette depicts the pharaoh Narmer on the reverse side, where he is using a piriform mace to smite a Libyan prisoner.[268] The mace is pointing up and the specific position of Narmer's arm, wrist, and hand suggests to some that the imminent blow would hit the side of the enemy's head, possibly either knocking it off or, perhaps more likely, caving it in.[269] This interpretation, unfortunately, does not take into account the "highly stylised nature of Egyptian art, which was specifically designed to enhance the clarity of the things represented rather than providing any kind of 'snapshot' of reality".[270]

The piriform mace is certainly used in smiting scenes throughout Dynastic Egypt. Not too long after the start of the Dynastic period (in relative terms) the mace was also employed in portrayals of 3rd Dynasty king Sekhemkhet at Wadi Maghara in the Sinai.[271] In such scenes the pharaoh, here wearing the White Crown, is depicted

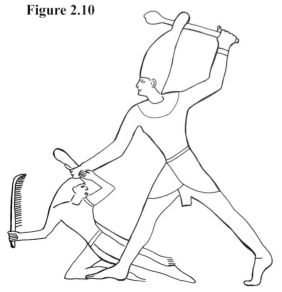

Figure 2.10

using a piriform mace to smite an Asiatic enemy.[272] The stylistic similarities between this particular depiction and earlier smiting scenes are very noticeable. A little bit further along the Dynastic timeline, at the end of the First Intermediate Period, pharaoh Montu-hotep II (also referred to as Mentuhotep II) is shown in a limestone relief from Gebelein, south of Thebes, preparing to smite a Libyan chieftain (identified by the feather held in his hand) **(Figure 2.10)**.[273] This particular image comes at an important time in Dynastic Egypt as, much like his early predecessor Narmer, Montu-hotep was responsible for overthrowing the Tenth Dynasty Herakleopolitan rulers[274] and re-uniting Egypt under one rule. Montu-hotep II was a very important figure in Dynastic Egypt's history and would have wanted to display his strength and authority in a traditional smiting scene as a time honoured way of exhibiting power.[275] Smiting scenes as a reflection of power were especially important at times of unification such as these.

A Middle Kingdom example of a smiting scene is found on a gold chest ornament (pectoral) depicting Amenemhat III smiting an enemy with a piriform mace in a pose almost identical to those seen in other smiting scenes with maces.[276] Even though maces began to appear less commonly in smiting scenes, such scenes themselves became more popular in the New Kingdom, occurring with increased regularity from the Eighteenth Dynasty reign of Thutmose III (Tuthmosis III) onwards.[277] Thutmose III himself uses a piriform mace in a smiting scene at Karnak, in which he holds his multiple victims by their hair in a pose of subjugation to display his power.[278]

This traditional depiction of power continued well into the Late Period and the Ptolemaic Period. The Macedonian Greek Ptolemies were determined to display themselves as legitimate pharaohs and continued the use of the mace as a powerful form of symbolism. One of the most arresting examples of this is Ptolemy XII

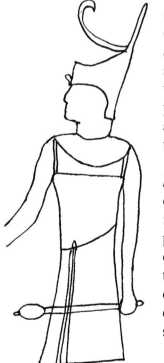

who had himself portrayed grasping the piriform mace to smite enemies on the front pylon gateway of the Temple of Horus at Edfu.[279] As Egypt's pre-eminent site of royal ancestor worship, the Ptolemaic pharaohs were keen to support the long-established ancient Egyptian religious traditions in an effort to secure the loyalty of Egypt's population, whilst at the same time employing the mace and smiting scene as a way of exhibiting their power and their supreme right to rule.[280]

Although other weapons were used (such as the *khopesh*), the mace (and the piriform mace in particular) certainly appears to have been the preferred weapon in many portrayals of smiting. This standard scene is a portrayal of ultimate royal supremacy and subjugation of the enemy awaiting imminent execution.[281] However, there appear to be few, if any, examples of the mace depicted in Egyptian portrayals of equal hand-to-hand combat as opposed to the execution style of the smiting scene.[282]

In Egyptian art the mace was included in religious

Figure 2.11

iconography from an early date, shown in scenes of siege warfare held in the talons of a falcon, overseeing the demolition of walled towns or fortifications.[283] In later religious iconography the mace was linked with divine fortifications and was even portrayed as the deity 'The Great White' in the Temple of Edfu texts.[284] The mace was also portrayed being used by the pharaoh, but as a method of displaying royal power outside of the traditional smiting scene. One such example is that of Hatshepsut, who was depicted as carrying a mace even before she became pharaoh, as can be seen in a carving on the north obelisk from Karnak[285] (**Figure 2.11**).

So it has become obvious to us that the mace as a weapon had various different uses and meanings. Not only was it a fairly effective clubbing and crushing blunt-force weapon, but it also held huge importance as a religious and pharaonic symbol of power. So powerful was its meaning that the mace as a weapon and a symbol continued almost completely unaltered (aside from a few interesting variations) from the very beginning of the developing Dynastic Egypt all the way through to the period of Roman rule. The importance of the mace in ancient Egyptian history cannot be stressed enough; it is one of the most vital aspects of the symbolism of pharaonic power.

Sword and Dagger

Sword

There were several types of swords in ancient Egypt. The *khopesh* (or *khepesh*) is the best-known of these swords and perhaps the most famous of all ancient Egyptian weapons, having often been featured in popular culture. There are examples of swords from the Middle Kingdom, cast as separate units, but these did not have the

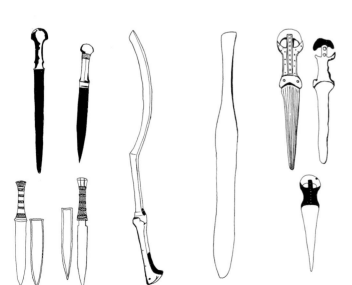

metal strength of the New Kingdom swords.[286] The sword became an important weapon in the New Kingdom. Before the innovations introduced under Hyksos rule, the sword was limited to a short blade resembling a long dagger. This dagger, usually double-edged and riveted, became widely used in the Middle Kingdom, as a close-range stabbing weapon.[287] Middle Kingdom daggers were tapered blades manufactured from copper

Figure 2.12

with short, wide handles featuring crescent-shaped pommels that would fit easily in the palm of a hand.[288] Whilst daggers were frequently carried on an arm-band, the sword was generally held on a belt wrapped around the soldier's waist, leading to distinctive wear patterns on the pommel of the long-sword.[289]

As with other weapons of the time, it is likely that the first blades were manufactured from copper or arsenical copper, before the transition to bronze in the manufacture of swords in the New Kingdom.[290] As mentioned with the axe-heads above, the addition of even the smallest amount of arsenic to the copper in the casting process would strengthen the blade a great deal.

The true sword in ancient Egypt was primarily a New Kingdom development, one made possible by the technological advances influenced by the period of Hyksos rule in the Second Intermediate Period.[291] At the start of the New Kingdom, a new dagger type began to be manufactured, one where the narrow blade and tang were cast all in one, which then went on to develop into what could almost be described as a short sword.[292] Early on in the New Kingdom, charioteers and infantry seemingly made use of short swords which were less than 70 cm in total length.[293] The Hyksos influence meant that the lenticular pommel of the earlier Egyptian dagger was replaced with a straight grip that was cast in one piece along with the blade, which therefore allowed the blade to be lengthened.[294]

An early Eighteenth Dynasty short sword housed in the Metropolitan Museum of Art, New York, is described as being an early stage of the development of its type of sword, as shown by its plain grip and blade and rounded point.[295] This particular sword is one cubit (20.5 in) in length and cast in a single piece with only traces of the original inlaid wooden plates from the grip remaining; the design and construction of this sword clearly show the Asiatic influence, paralleling earlier short swords of Asiatic design.[296] Long (straight) swords with tapered tangs were later able to be fashioned due to the further metallurgical developments of the New Kingdom.[297] Ancient Egypt was apparently dependent on copper for weaponry longer than other contemporary societies.[298] However, once the development of bronze as the primary metal for weapons manufacture took place, the longer sword blades were strengthened so they were suitable for military use.[299] As mentioned above, the blade and handle of these longer swords could be cast in one single piece (known as the Naue II type) and their development coincided with the rise of armoured infantry in the region.[300]

The long tangs cast with the blade ensured that the swords had reasonable levels of stability as during combat the stress points were predominantly focussed on the hilt.[301] When straight swords were created for elite soldiers they would often be inscribed with the cartouche of the reigning pharaoh, meaning that when the sword pierced an enemy all the power and presence of the pharaoh was meant to be felt.[302] This point also has considerable relevance for the weapons found in the tomb of Ahhotep; although inscribed with the names of her sons, kings Kamose and Ahmose, this is not necessarily indicative that the weapons belonged to these men rather than Ahhotep herself as is sometimes suggested.

Along with the long (or straight) sword there was also a long, leaf-shaped sword that was developed which was cast with either a plain or a crescent-shaped pommel.[303] A number of examples of this type of sword have been found at the city of Amarna.[304] This leaf-shaped blade was also seen on New Kingdom examples of knives, including one example from el Lisht, where the double-edged blade was fashioned to look like a laurel leaf.[305]

Moving on from the straight sword form, the *khopesh* was a weapon that resembled a scimitar, with a curved blade generally believed to have been modelled on an Asiatic weapon first seen in the Second Intermediate Period under Hyksos rule.[306] It is possibly that its name derives from the *khopesh* joint, specifically the right foreleg of an ox that was cut off and used for meat offerings to deities in Egyptian rituals.[307] It was the Hyksos who supposedly introduced the *khopesh* into Egypt, along with the relevant body armour and helmets (and the previously mentioned chariot). They quite possibly unwittingly provided the Egyptians with the means by which they eventually defeated the Hyksos rulers.[308] It is possible that the manufacturing techniques for the *khopesh* came from Canaan, although there may also have been direct imports through either trade or tribute.[309] Examples of this are shown in reliefs in early Theban tombs, in which foreigners are depicted with the *khopesh* and the straight sword as objects of tribute.[310]

The *khopesh* blade is wedge-shaped (widening at the back) with the cutting edge on the outer edge of the blade, as in the case of the scimitar blade,[311] and functioned as a long and thin, almost axe-like weapon.[312] Indeed, by the end of the Eighteenth Dynasty, the *khopesh* had replaced the axe as one of the most important weapons in the Egyptian military.[313] The Egyptian army used different sizes of *khopesh* swords for different purposes on the battlefield, as shown by the *khopesh* swords found in the tomb of Tutankhamun.[314]

Two particularly excellent examples of the *khopesh* were found in the

Figure 2.13

aforementioned burial goods of Tutankhamun.[315] Designating them as offensive weapons,[316] Howard Carter names them as bronze falchions; one large and heavy example being found amongst the single sticks (Figure 2.13) and the smaller and lighter one was found on the floor with other miscellaneous objects.[317] Carter theorises that the smaller sword (16 in long; 40.6 cm) was made for Tutankhamun when he was a child and that the larger weapon (23.5 in long; 59.7 cm) was most likely made for the pharaoh when adolescent.[318] In the case of both weapons, the blade, the shaft, and the handle-piece were all cast in one single piece with a handle-plate fitted with ebony side plates.[319]

The larger of the two swords (the model for the *khopesh* employed in the experimental archaeology) would appear to have been designed for crushing rather than cutting, as the convex cutting edge was only partially developed.[320] This larger *khopesh* would have inflicted serious wounds due to the sheer weight of the blade (rather than any real sharpness).[321] This sort of weapon was certainly designed to create blunt-force-trauma damage on the battlefield, opening gaps in an enemy's armour.[322] The smaller *khopesh*, less curved than the larger one, had a shaper edge more like that of a knife.[323] The cutting edge was finely honed and sharpened and would have been more effective at thrusting, cutting and slicing lightly armoured enemies.[324] There is an assumption that this smaller *khopesh* was made for Tutankhamun as a child but this is not necessarily accurate; the smaller *khopesh* could potentially have been a weapon designed for adult use, perhaps for combat practice.

Depictions of these different sword types varied. Both deities and pharaohs are often portrayed armed with swords and the long-sword tended to be shown in active combat scenes, particularly in reliefs of siege operations.[325] Further scenes, especially from the reign of Ramesses II, show the soldiers executing prisoners by striking them through the throat or chest with a straight sword, examples of which can be found in the reliefs portraying both the siege at Ashkelon and the Battle of Kadesh.[326] There are also examples of the pharaoh driving a chariot whilst simultaneously wielding a *khopesh* sword. One of these depicts Seti I in battle with the Libyans, in which he holds his chariot reins in his left hand and the *khopesh* in his right as he prepares to decapitate the Libyan chief.[327]

One of the earliest examples of the portrayal of soldiers using swords is found at Deir el-Bahri, in Hatshepsut's mortuary temple; here duelling soldiers are depicted using short *khopesh* swords.[328] These weapons, however, were most likely carved from wood rather than made from bronze as they would have been used in a ceremonial context, such as sword-play during the funeral rites of a pharaoh. These ceremonial swords often had a looped handle attached, enabling them to be held on the wrist when necessary.[329]

The *khopesh* seemed to be reserved for non-combat situations, being used more

in processional or ceremonial scenes rather
than those which depict violent contact; the
pharaoh's bowmen and bodyguards, for
example, are often depicted as being armed
with the *khopesh*.[330] The *khopesh* often
features in the most important symbolic
scenes such as smiting, pharaoh driving
a chariot into battle, hunting scenes and
scenes portraying the dismemberment of
enemy prisoners.[331] The limited variation in
portrayal of the *khopesh* could well be due
to the fact that it is a slashing weapon and
did not fit into Egyptian artistic conventions
where depicting movement was generally
avoided.[332]

Yet one of the most crucial representations of
the *khopesh* in relation to this book is an example
of the *khopesh* wielded by a woman. This particular depiction
was found on a limestone block that was originally part
of a temple scene from Amarna.[333] The relief represents a

Figure 2.14

traditional ancient Egyptian smiting scene and shows Nefertiti as reigning monarch,
standing on a royal barge wielding a *khopesh* against a female foreign prisoner[334]
(**Figure 2.14**). In this scene, Nefertiti is stripped to the waist and is wearing the
ceremonial male-style kilt of the pharaoh. This is an outfit appropriate for the act
that she is about to carry out, an act that is traditionally the domain of the pharaoh.[335]

Dagger

The dagger was a hugely important weapon for the ancient Egyptians during both
the Predynastic and Dynastic periods. In Pre- and Early Dynastic times, the dagger
was generally a straight copper blade; this had either a midrib or no midrib and
was usually set into a hilt that had curving projections that enclosed the top of
the blade.[336] As with the majority of weapons manufactured and used in Egypt,
the dagger was generally made of bronze (particularly from the New Kingdom
onwards), a metal which continued to be used long after other nations had adopted
iron or steel.[337]

The dagger is often depicted in tomb and temple wall scenes and many examples
have been found in archaeological contexts.[338] The design for the dagger appears
to have remained fairly consistent throughout the Bronze Age, as did the copper
alloys from which daggers were manufactured.[339] The dagger became more widely
used as a weapon for stabbing and crushing the enemy at close quarters from the

Middle Kingdom onwards.[340] The Hyksos introduced a new type of dagger, one which had two-edged blade with a midrib.[341] This then led on to the introduction of new weapon-production techniques during the New Kingdom, which enabled narrower and sharper dagger blades to be made.[342] This also allowed the dagger to evolve into a weapon that resembled a short sword at the beginning of the New Kingdom when the narrow blade and tang were cast in one go.[343]

A Middle Kingdom dagger was found in the Twelfth Dynasty burial of Senebtisi, whose mummy was buried with a set of weapons that were described as magical; they were intended to be talismans for Senebtisi going on her journey into the afterlife.[344] This is a reference to ceremonial, non-combat staves and the somewhat less ceremonial dagger which had a wooden sheath, partially overlaid with gold foil.[345] Senebtisi's dagger conforms to the general design of the majority of Middle Kingdom daggers which often had a tapered copper blade, an elaborate short and wide hilt, and a characteristic crescent-shaped pommel.[346] Her dagger could have been used as a functioning weapon, although this has not been archaeologically proven.

In relation to the dagger within the army, the Egyptians classified their military according to the arms carried by the different regiments.[347] There were Archer regiments, Lancer regiments and the Spearmen, some of the Lancers also carrying a dagger tucked in their belts in addition to their lances (or pikes).[348] It is possible that most soldiers also carried a dagger, possibly as a weapon of last resort.

During the period of Hyksos rule we have more information about the style of weapons which were in use. One such example is an Asiatic style inlaid silver-hilted bronze dagger found in the tomb of the male official, Abdu, at Saqqara.[349] This dagger was inscribed with the Hyksos and Egyptian names of Apophis Nebkhopeshre, one of the Hyksos pharaohs, and possibly the 'King Apophis' known to have been the opponent of Theban pharaoh Kamose in the early stages of the development of the New Kingdom.[350]

Another example of a Hyksos dagger was purchased from a Luxor dealer in 1916 by a member of the British military, but there is unfortunately no provenance attached to the weapon[351] (although a southern Egyptian find-spot seems likely). The dagger has a total length of 41.3 cm, a handle length of 12.2 cm, a semi-circular top of the handle width of 5 cm, and a base of handle shoulder width of 4 cm.[352] It would appear that the handle was originally inlaid, although there is no evidence of rivet-holes that would have held the handle in place; the blade itself has a mid-rib that runs down the entire length of the blade and the whole surface of the dagger is eroded and is covered in green corrosion.[353] One particularly interesting aspect of this dagger was the cartouche inscribed on the right side of the blade, very close to where it joined the hilt; the cartouche displays the prenomen of Hyksos king Apophis 'Okenenrē', possibly a contemporary of Theban king Seqenenre Tao of the Seventeenth Dynasty,[354] and believed to be Kamose's father.

One particularly elaborate dagger often suggested as being a ceremonial weapon was found in the tomb of Seqenenre's chief wife, Queen Ahhotep, along with the axes previously mentioned.[355] This dagger was decorated with the name of the pharaoh Ahmose I,[356] second son of Ahhotep. The dagger blade is decorated with an image of a lion hunting a calf, the lion in the so-called 'flying gallop' pose.[357] The blade is also decorated on the same side with four grasshoppers or locusts and, although the significance of this is not generally understood,[358] some theories suggest that the insects represent the Egyptian people.[359]

Jánosi also believes the dagger design incorporates Aegean elements, particularly in the simplified design of the landscape above the animals.[360] The dagger has other features that make it stand out compared to contemporary examples: the joint between the blade and the hilt is fashioned from a bull's head of gold and at the top of the hilt is a pommel that displays four female heads, one on each side.[361]

More well-known Eighteenth Dynasty daggers are the two elaborate examples that were found within the wrappings of the mummy of Tutankhamen. The first of these can be assumed to be ceremonial in design[362] and was found underneath one of the girdles placed around the waist of the mummy.[363] It measures 31.9 cm in length and has a blade of gold.[364] The hilt was particularly ornate, comprising alternating bands of granulated gold and cloisonné bands of lapis lazuli, carnelian, malachite, and glass, and there are cartouches (of Tutankhamun) on top of the hilt that are made of applied embossed gold, a red tinge to the gold suggesting it was hardened with the addition of copper.[365] The dagger sheath is also very decorative, made of sheet gold delicately inlaid with a hunting scene on the back resembling the standard hunting scenes found on contemporary tomb walls.[366]

The second Tutankhamun dagger is perhaps a more unusual example, its blade made of iron making it relatively heavy in comparison to the majority of daggers from this period, which were generally made from bronze.[367] This dagger was again found in the mummy wrappings, held in place along the right thigh of the pharaoh.[368] The hilt of this dagger is similar to the hilt of the gold one but this iron dagger has an unusual pommel made of rock crystal,[369] recalling the crystal mace head of Senebtisi (discussed above). The sheath of this dagger is also made from sheet gold and decorated with a feathered *rishi* pattern.[370]

This iron dagger was quite possibly a gift from the Hittites, as Anatolia is alleged to have been one of the first places where iron production occurred.[371] Certainly in the Eighteenth or Nineteenth Dynasty, a Hittite monarch was corresponding with a neighbour with regard to iron that the latter wanted and providing him with blades for iron daggers. It is thought that this neighbour is in fact Ramesses II but as the names of both the addressee and his country are lost (as well as those of the sender and his country) a fair amount of supposition is involved.[372] However, there is also evidence that the dagger may have come from another source; there is apparently some resemblance between this dagger and those sent to the Eighteenth Dynasty pharaoh Amenhotep III by the Mitanni ruler Tushratta.[373] The location of the western Asian Mitannian state, located in the area of the Tigris and Euphrates rivers,[374] meant that they were well located to serve as an intermediary trader between the Egyptians to the south and the northerly Hittites.

As daggers were not a major combat weapon in battle, their depiction is perhaps not as prevalent as those of other weapons. Generally, there are just brief glimpses of the dagger in reliefs. For example, the portrayal of a battle-scene at Deshasheh depicts an officer watching the sappers at work whilst he leans on a staff and appears to have a dagger stuck in his belt.[375] One of the few royal depictions of battle dated to the Old Kingdom, and found in the reliefs on the Fifth Dynasty funerary causeway of Unas, portrays a clash between an Asiatic soldier and several Egyptians armed with daggers, bows, and arrows.[376]

Nonetheless, the dagger was often depicted attached to the kilt of the pharaoh and presumably placed there for use as a weapon of last resort when all other means had failed.[377] One depiction of the dagger in this form comes from one of two relief fragments acquired for the British Museum; the smaller of these pieces depicts a king most likely to be identified as Montu-hotep II and his princess daughter, Ioh, priestess of Hathor.[378] The king is identified through his costume, consisting of the white crown of Upper Egypt and a short tunic with a girdle that supported both a pendant tail and a dagger.[379] As the pharaoh carried other weapons (a mace and a long sceptre), albeit possibly ceremonial ones, this shows how the dagger was not a primary weapon but a secondary, or even tertiary, one.[380] The practice of wearing the dagger at the waist is also found in the case of women; the princess Ita buried wearing a bronze dagger at her waist.[381]

Spear

Spears are often found in ancient Egyptian burials. Some examples of late spear-heads are held in the Harrogate Museum. The spear was one of the primary weapons used in the Predynastic Period (along with the axe, mace, and simple bow).[382] The spear must be one of the most basic weapons in ancient civilisations – think how easy it would be for even the earliest humans to carve a wooden stick into a sharp point and to then throw it at an enemy. It would then make sense for early humans and civilisations to try and improve on the basic design as time went on, particularly when civilisations developed metallurgy and therefore the ability to add sharp metal to their pointy sticks. Presumably the earliest spears in what became ancient Egypt were of the pointed wooden stick kind, before developing in the metal spear-heads we see later on.

One excellent resource for looking at spears in the Dynastic period are the model soldiers found in the Eleventh Dynasty (Middle Kingdom) tomb of Mehseti **(Figure**

Figure 2.15

2.15). These extraordinary little models depict forty Egyptian spearmen (and forty Nubian archers) in exquisite detail.[383] The spears are as tall as the soldiers (although each soldiers seems to hold their spear at a different height), with wooden shafts and long leaf-shaped bronze spear-heads,[384] a common spear-head shape that is used even in the Late Period, as seen in some examples from the Harrogate Museum. This spear-head was most likely attached to the wooden shaft via the spear-head tang, as was common in the Old and Middle Kingdoms.[385] In this time, the blades were mostly composed of copper or bronze[386] depending on how well developed the ancient Egyptians' metallurgy techniques were.

By the time of the New Kingdom, however, the spear-heads were attached via the use of socket that formed part of the blade and was pushed onto the top of the wooden shaft.[387] Whether or not the attachments were strengthened by the use of reed or leather ties is not really known, as reed and animal hide do not survive too well in the archaeological record. It would make sense, though, for some sort of tie to be used, as evidenced by some of the axes found in Egypt with remnants of reed and hide and as seen with the replica axe created for the experimental archaeology I carried out.

Along with the more conventional spear-head design (one intended for throwing at an enemy), there was also a type that resembled a halberd more than a traditional spear.[388] Again, this would generally be made of copper or bronze and seemed to be more designed as a hacking and slashing weapon, not dissimilar to the axe and the sword from the same period.[389] As with any other ancient civilisation, the general design and engineering of the spear remained fairly consistent throughout Dynastic Egypt with some relatively small variations and deviations (the halberd design aside).

Stave and Throw-stick

Staves, or quarterstaves, are relatively simple weapons that are sometimes depicted in ancient Egyptian art and are also at times found in tomb goods, such as those found in the tomb of Senebtisi or the staves found (along with axes, bows, and arrows) in the Eleventh Dynasty (Middle Kingdom) tomb of Meket-Re, High Steward to Pharaoh Se'ankh-ku-Re Montu-hotep III.[390] Staves (also referred to as staffs) were sometimes used as tokens of office by various court and bureaucratic officials, but obviously I am going to concentrate on the military versions here. The straight stave is similar in style to the quarterstaff so popular in Medieval Britain and were generally 4-5 ft in length.[391] The use of the stave as a weapon is found in carvings from the Old Kingdom, such as the Fifth Dynasty depiction of Egyptian soldiers carrying staves (as well as axes and bows) found at el-Lisht.[392] Most examples of the staves found in the archaeological record are thought to be ceremonial in nature, generally found in the burial goods of courtiers or other nobles.[393]

There are some examples of New Kingdom burials containing staves, particularly those during the reigns of the Thutmoside pharaohs, where the staves seemingly functioned as both weapons and walking sticks/badges of office.[394] However, it would seem that the majority of staves/staffs were ceremonial is nature and that they would not have been used all that often in active combat. It could be that any depictions of soldiers carrying staves were portraying military ceremonies, not battle situations.

Throw-sticks also have similarities with the staves, in that they were not exclusively for military use. Similar in style, engineering and use to the boomerangs used by Indigenous Australians, the recurved projectile[395] (not designed for returning, unlike the boomerang) seems to have been primarily used in the hunting of waterfowl and other small animals, although there were occasions when they were used by soldiers.[396] Whilst these throw-sticks may have brought down birds with relative ease, it is difficult to imagine them doing a huge amount of damage to a grown man such as an enemy soldier.

The weapons used by the ancient Egyptians were incredible in their design and just how many different types of weaponry they developed, especially considering it was an ancient civilisation without the technological advancements of the current day. Although there was little variation within each weapon type, any technological changes (such as the move from stone to copper, from copper to bronze, and the development of the self/simple bow into the composite bow) were always with the aim of improving the effectiveness of the weapon. The ancient Egyptians were more than willing to borrow such improvements from other civilisations (such as the chariot and the composite bow from the Hyksos), but also made improvements of their own. The Egyptians became such a powerful civilisation, with a huge empire at one point, due to not only the machinations of their rulers but also the might of the military (particularly in the New Kingdom) and the advancements made in their weaponry.

Future Research

Though a great deal of research has been carried out on ancient Egyptian weaponry, and indeed the Egyptian military in general, there are still areas where the subject is lacking. One problem with work previously done on weaponry and warfare is a lack of analysis into the weapons and the soldiers who wielded them. There remains a distinct dearth of scientific application in the study of ancient Egyptian warfare, which is perplexing when scientific analysis plays such a major role in other aspects of Egyptian archaeology. There has been little experimental archaeology carried out, with one notable example being undertaken by Thomas Hulit and Thom Richardson[397] examining scale armour, archery, and chariots from the New Kingdom. Yet what has been done is rarely mentioned in any of the resources available on the subject of ancient Egyptian weaponry. Most scholars seem to prefer to rely on written sources and/or artistic evidence alone, with little attempt to combine these resources with the practical aspects of archaeology. There absolutely needs to be more scientific work done on the subject, such as experimental archaeology and other forms of scientific analysis. Think about how much more we could learn about these ancient Egyptian weapons (including how there were used, the sort of trauma they would cause, and just how effective they were) if we tested them more thoroughly.

As we have seen, a significant problem encountered within Egyptian archaeology is the issue of women associated with warfare. This has been a somewhat controversial subject in the past and there are times when the fact that women were at all associated with combat in any way, shape, or form is completely ignored. Spalinger (2005) for example makes few references to Hatshepsut other than oblique references to her military campaigns, but his work overwhelmingly focuses on male pharaohs. Indeed, the title of this work '*War in Ancient Egypt*' is not completely accurate, as it concentrates almost exclusively on the Eighteenth Dynasty. Spalinger also makes no mention whatsoever of Nefertiti (except for a brief reference to the marriage of Horemheb to a woman some believe to have been Nefertiti's sister[398]) despite the clear pictorial evidence she participated in some form of military activity, i.e. the smiting scene relief from Amarna. Nor is there any reference to Ahhotep, despite the significant written and artefactual evidence pointing to the queen's participation in active warfare.

By no means is Spalinger the only academic guilty of this tendency to omit such information. Many scholars fail to acknowledge that women were involved with warfare and weapons within Egyptian society, unless to dismiss any such involvement as a 'symbolic' occurrence. Although I in no way wish to suggest that women were frequently involved in warfare it can be demonstrated that it did occur from time to time and often with startling, albeit rare, examples. Wilfully ignoring this fact is unproductive and means that an important element is lacking in the study of ancient Egyptian practices.

3

Defending Ancient Egypt

Public Defence: Fortresses

When examining warfare and weaponry in ancient Egypt we need to look at defence as well as offence. The defence of Egypt and its soldiers took various forms, including defensive building works (such as fortresses, walls, and border posts), the use of personal shields by soldiers, and, arguably, through political manoeuvres by Egypt's rulers. One of ancient Egypt's largest defensive projects was the building of border fortresses. There were several examples of these built throughout Dynastic Egypt's history on the orders of several pharaohs. One of the most famous Pharaohs, Ramesses II, ordered the building of a line of such fortresses along Egypt's north-western coast in a bid to prevent further infiltrations into his lands by the 'Sea Peoples'.[399]

As previously discussed, prior to the New Kingdom, Egypt usually had a policy of defending its existing borders rather than looking outwards at the state's geographical and political expansion. As a result of this particular outlook, Egypt had no standing army, but instead relied almost exclusively on provincial militias and conscription when threatened with invasion.[400] One example of this took place in the Sixth Dynasty (during the reign of Pepi I) when an attempted invasion by the 'sand-dwellers' or 'Shasu' threatened his eastern borders. The force raised by Pepi I was led by Weni, a court official with no previous military leadership experience. With numbers on his side Weni's lack of experience was overcome, leading to a successful outcome for Egypt. Due to this Weni was then appointed as the army commander for at least four more operations against the 'sand-dwellers'.[401] It would seem that Pepi I was perfectly content to leave his army's activities at defensive manoeuvres and had no desire, and perhaps no resources, to expand Egypt's borders at that time.[402] So did Old Kingdom military/defence attitudes influence the building of fortresses? Fortresses certainly do not seem to have been designed specifically for outward invasions.

Fortresses (rather than fortified towns) were built by the ancient Egyptians in order to guard and control Egypt's vulnerable northern and southern frontiers. These, primarily mudbrick, structures could hold up to a few hundred troops (occasionally comprising Nubian, Philistine, or Libyan soldiers), serving for up to six years at a time.[403] According to the Semna Papyri (reports that were sent by the commander of the fortress at Semna to the military headquarters at Thebes during the reign of Amenemhat III), these troops had to carry out surveillance and reconnaissance patrols of the surrounding areas at regular intervals.[404] There were examples of fortresses (called the Walls of the Prince) that were built in the eastern Delta during the reign of Amenemhat I (1991-1962BC), which were designed to defend the coastal route from the Levant.[405] This was at around the same time as a fortress was built at Wadi Natrun, which was designed to defend the western Delta region against invading Libyans. These sites were maintained and improved during the New Kingdom, perhaps as a way to prevent reinvasion by the Hyksos, who had ruled this area of Egypt in the Second Intermediate Period between the Middle Kingdom and the New Kingdom.[406]

The mudbrick fortress of Buhen, in Lower Nubia (in the Second Cataract, 156 miles upstream of Aswan[407]), is one of the most well-known and impressive of these structures. Buhen was one of the most elaborate of ancient Egypt's fortresses and united all the Second Cataract fortresses under its command by the time of the New Kingdom.[408] Initially founded in the Second Dynasty, the site was established early on as a trade centre, becoming known for copper-smelting in the Fourth and Fifth Dynasties. It was during the Middle Kingdom that the fortress was enlarged and strengthened in order to become a frontier fortress, one of a string of eleven in the area.[409] These improvements took the form of mudbrick ramparts added to the 4m thick outer western wall, which itself incorporated five large towers. There was also a large central tower that served as the main entrance (comprising two openings with double wooden doors) and a drawbridge.[410] The inner fortress was built along a more regular square plan and had towers at each corner along with bastions that were at 5-metre intervals.[411]

While fortresses always played a defensive role to some extent, there are many interpretations as to their core role, both in terms of function and symbolism. Shaw is of the opinion that these Nubian fortresses were not designed for border defence but were, in fact, to protect Egypt's monopoly on exotic trade goods (such as gold and ivory) which were brought up through Nubia into Egypt.[412] Archaeologists generally believe that fortresses such as Buhen were designed for propaganda reasons, with elaborate crenellations, bastions, and ditches. As Buhen was built on flat ground with a square ground-plan it would have looked very impressive but, arguably, would have been difficult to defend effectively as it lacked any advantage, such as being built on top of a hill or other elevated land.[413] Certainly by the New Kingdom, Buhen had become a primarily civilian settlement, as Egypt's frontiers were pushed further south.[414]

Arguments on their exact role aside, the importance of fortresses cannot be ignored and the erection of new fortresses (or rather forts and walls) continues long throughout the New Kingdom and beyond. Some of the most notable include the string of forts along the Mediterranean coast of the Delta that were commissioned by Ramesses II and the forts at Qasr Ibrim and Qasr Qarun that were built by the Roman rulers in the Graeco-Roman Period of Egypt's history.[415] During periods of great disturbance (such as the Third Intermediate Period and the Late Period) there was an increase in the building of fortifications. The Kushite King Piye even boasted on his stele at Gebel Barkal of his defeat of the Egyptians in 734BC, which includes a mention of Middle Egypt and its nineteen fortified settlements along with various walled cities in the Egyptian Delta.[416] This boasting by Piye shows the importance of fortresses in the defence of ancient Egypt, at least in the minds of Egypt's enemies.

Personal Protection: Shields

While the fortresses of ancient Egypt no doubt played an important role in the defence of the country, warfare and fighting more often occurred on battlefields and open ground. As such the personal protection of the soldiers in battle was one of the most important elements of defence for Ancient Egyptians.

Early scholarly work that looked at ancient Egyptian warfare was often biased (particularly in relation defence and armour), relying on a general view of the ancient world instead of using actual archaeological evidence. Some scholars based their work entirely on the descriptions of Herodotus (Boutelle 1893)[417] or even cited no evidence at all, be that historical or archaeological (Ellacott 1962).[418] While it has taken a while to catch up, the discipline has moved forwards greatly with recent work examining, and dispelling, such inaccuracies.

Even as early as the Predynastic period, Egyptian foot soldiers often carried an arch-topped shield made from some sort of animal hide (usually cow-hide). This would be stretched over a wooden frame, covering the soldier approximately from their head to their knee (between 1 m and 1.5 m in length).[419] Shield handles would be carved out of the centre of the shield's wooden framework or could be attached via the use of a wooden handle-bar stitched across the centre of the shield body (**Figure 3.1**).[420] It has also been theorised that leather straps could be attached to the shield handle, enabling

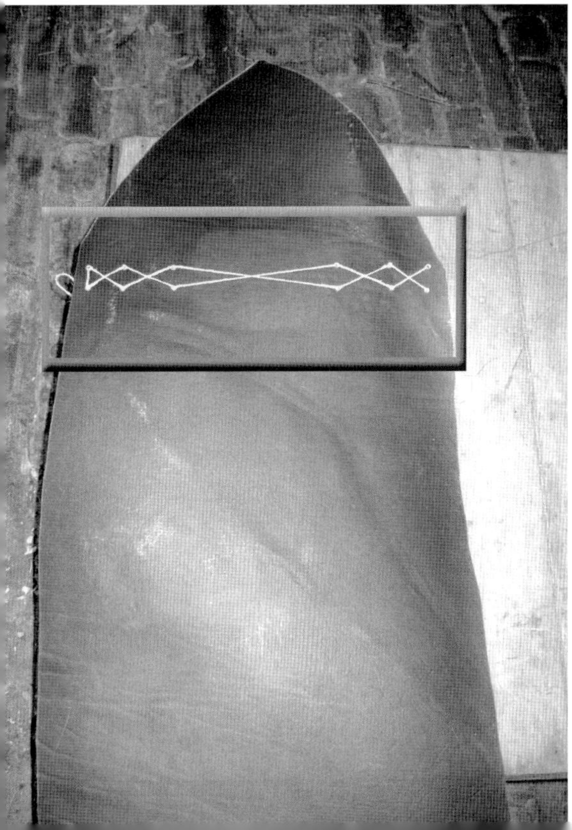

Figure 3.1

the shield to be carried across the shoulder and ensuring both hands could be left free.[421]

Shields were used from the late Predynastic period and were the most commonly portrayed defensive item throughout Dynastic Egypt.[422] Very few actual ancient Egyptian shields have survived in the archaeological record, which somewhat limits what we can find out about their construction and the materials they were made from. This is particularly true of the shields from the Old and Middle Kingdoms[423] as we currently have not found any complete shields from these periods. As such there are several different interpretations that have arisen regarding shields as a result of the lack of concrete archaeological evidence or information.[424]

Even something as simple as size is not known for certain with shields of this age, though there is a general consensus among many academics. Shaw states that the Old and Middle Kingdom shields were made in two sizes: either 1 m or 1.5 m in height.[425] McDermott's shield-size hypothesis is similar to Shaw's with the addition of a very large shield designed for use in sieges.[426] McDermott believes that this large shield would be operated by several men and may have been developed in the Middle Kingdom but abandoned later due to its sheer unwieldiness.[427] Hayes' appraisal of the usual Old and Middle Kingdom shield sizes conforms to those of Shaw and McDermott.[428]

These larger shields can also be seen in tomb paintings at el-Bersha, though it is pointed out that it is uncertain as to whether or not such large shields were really used in battle by Egyptian soldiers.[429] Such shields are apparently absent from the

battle scenes at Beni Hasan and Stonborough theorises that these types of shields, rather than being functional warfare and defensive items, may have actually been symbolic or religious in character.[430] However, Stonborough also points out that if these large shields were to be used in battle they were probably designed to protect several men at once, likely from airborne projectiles such as arrows.[431] He argues that such shields were unwieldy in melee fighting due to their sheer size, and would probably have made the carrying and use of weapons near-impossible whilst holding such a shield.[432] This can be seen in one of the paintings at the site of el-Bersha, where one of the soldiers carrying a man-sized shield is not holding a weapon[433] **(Figure 3.2)**.

One of the best sources for information on the ancient Egyptian shields is commonly acknowledged to be found amongst the burial goods from the Eleventh Dynasty tomb of Mehseti, a provincial governor. Uncovered at Asyut these artefacts included two painted wooden models of

Figure 3.2

Figure 3.3

groups of soldiers.[434] These little models depict in almost perfect detail the soldiers' dress, weapons and shields – the spearmen models hold a beautifully painted shield (designed to emulate the cow-hides from which the shield body was taken) in their left hands and a spear in their right hands[435] **(Figures 3.3 and 3.4)**.

When it comes to the pattern and design of the shields in ancient Egypt, in the Old and Middle Kingdoms most of the shield depictions show a surface design of mottled cow hair. This can also be seen clearly on the shields of Mehseti's model

soldiers.[436] It has been suggested by Hayes that the ancient Egyptians left the hair on the hides they used when making shields; the argument is that leaving the hair on the hides contributed to their resilience, aiding in the deflection of projectile and other close blows, such as those from close-quarter fighting.[437]

Stonborough certainly finds it unlikely that the ancient Egyptians would have gone to such lengths as de-hairing the

Figure 3.4

cow hides only to then decorate the shields in the same cow-hide patterns.[438] He suggests that the hides were just de-fleshed and then left to dry out naturally in the air which, as his 2011 experiments (discussed later in the book) suggest, produces a light, rigid, and strong hide.[439] Ideal for shield manufacture! This light hide would have been vulnerable to moisture-induced decay, but as he points out, this would not have particularly been a problem in ancient Egypt where there was such an arid climate.[440] This type of decay may well by why so few Old and Middle Kingdom shields survive; it is certainly what has been suggested with regards to the examples of rawhide scale armour which have been found.[441]

When the generalities of shield-making are not entirely certain it is none-too-surprising that there is debate over the details. Some academics claim that the shields were made of cow-hides stretched over a wooden framework with a handle carved directly into the centre.[442] Hayes, on the other hand, suggests that the shields comprised of just a single sheet of cowhide with no wooden frame at all, the only wooden element of the shield being a wooden crossbar with a carved handle.[443] The theory put forward by Hayes comes from his study of some shield fragments from an expedition by the Metropolitan Museum of Art in New York,[444] but his findings are hard to corroborate as the expedition is not named and it seems as though the shield fragments have not survived into the present day.[445]

Despite the disappearance of these shield fragments mentioned by Hayes, Stonborough states that the existence of crossbars is not in doubt.[446] He argues that three examples survive in the Metropolitan Museum of Art in New York and did in fact feature in Hayes' work on Middle Kingdom Egypt.[447] One of the crossbars was so large that it has been suggested it goes some way to proving the existence of the huge man-encompassing shields discussed above, although this has yet to be verified.[448] The other two crossbars, however, were of a more manageable size, probably intended to protect an individual soldier in combat.[449] These smaller crossbars apparently showed no sign of being part of a wooden frame or backing, something that, Stonborough argues, substantiates Hayes' theory on shield construction.[450] This would also seem to be backed-up by the shields of the model soldiers from Mesehti's tomb, which exhibit only a crossbar with handle on their reverse[451]. According to Stonborough's analysis, the way Mesehti's wooden soldiers hold their shields clearly show how these crossbars would have functioned.[452]

The way in which the crossbar would have been attached to the body of the shield is still under debate as there are several possibilities apparent when images and models of shields were examined.[453] The shields that form part of the Mesehti models do not show any detail as to how the crossbars were attached. Stonbrorough suggests that some form of adhesive may have been used as the ancient Egyptians did use glues (made from either animals or plant gums)[454] for other tasks. There may be some questions as to how the adhesive would hold up under constant use (whilst they may have been effective, they were hardly modern-day superglue!), but without further testing and experimentation it is difficult to know just how well the glue would have lasted. While no traces of glue are mentioned by Hayes when he discusses the crossbars held in the Metropolitan Museum, it is unlikely that any analysis of these crossbars was actually carried out in order to determine if there were any adhesive traces present.[455]

On close examination of the Mesehti models it has been suggested that ties holding the crossbars onto the main body of the shield are another possible solution; and a small number of the models display a line of large and irregular cross-stitching on the front of the shields that generally follows the line of the crossbar located on the other side of the shield face[456] **(Figure 3.5)**. Stonborough is of the belief that these lines of cross-stitching represent strings or ties (possibly made of leather or reed) that held the crossbars to the main shield body. Such an interpretation seems to be backed-up by the smaller Metropolitan Museum

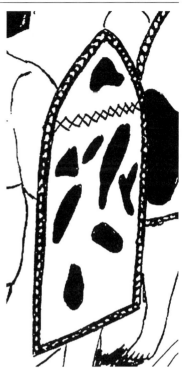

Figure 3.5

crossbars, both of which display evidence of small grooves carved into them on the handle side.[457] These were possibly used as guidelines for the strings when attaching the crossbar to the shield body using this particular method.

There is just one small problem with this method of attaching the crossbar to the main body of the shield. Stonborough points out that the use of ties alone to attach the crossbar would have been potentially extremely dangerous in the midst of battle. Just one blow to the ties could sever them, leading to the detachment of the crossbar from the shield making it as good as useless in the heat of battle.[458] One theory put forward is that the method of tying the crossbar to the shield with leather or reeds was one born out of necessity, a temporary measure, for example when the crossbar had come loose during a campaign and there was no adhesive available for use.[459] Then again, why would an army on campaign not take what could be described as essential repair supplies with them? Another possibility is that both strings and adhesive were used to secure the crossbars on together, though whether this would be a relatively permanent method, or a quick fix for battlefield damage, is currently impossible to establish.

By the time we reach the New Kingdom, there were changes in the design of the shields. Gradually they became a more rounded shape, with the ends sometimes being shown as narrower than their midsection, and the addition of a convex

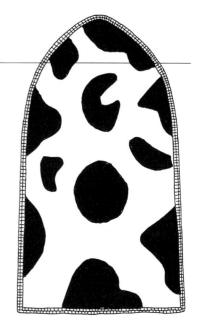

boss.[460] It is not certain whether or not these changes in appearance also included changes in the materials used to make the shields, but it has been argued that in the New Kingdom shields were in fact composed of wood which would either be covered in animal hide or painted in a black and tan design[461] **(Figure 3.6)**. It is dangerous to rush into such assumptions however as it is possible that this suggested change is based purely upon shields found in Tutankhamun's tomb; these shields were likely to have been made for display rather than combat. As such caution must be taken when generalising too greatly towards the shields actually used by soldiers in combat at this time.[462]

Figure 3.6

Tutankhamun's eight shields are the only mostly complete shields that have been found in Egypt and are examples of superb craftsmanship. All of them are made of wood, with the four larger ones featuring gilded wood openwork.[463] The four smaller shields are comprised of three wooden panels fixed together and are covered with valuable, fragile materials including cheetah and antelope hides.[464] They also have gilded gesso panels that are inscribed with the pharaoh's nomen and prenomen. Such details, combined with the fragile hide coverings, make it unlikely that these were ever intended for use in combat/ actual warfare.[465] The same can be said for the four larger shields as well, their openwork is certainly not appropriate for use in combat and would likely shatter at any blow from a weapon, leaving the wielder without any defence. It is therefore most likely that that the shields used in actual combat were very different in construction, if not in style, to those found in Tutankhamun's tomb.

It is possible that the developments in weaponry in the New Kingdom were responsible for the changes in shield design that are seen in this period. The introduction of the *khopesh* (the curved sword) and the composite bow by the Hyksos, among others, could have resulted in this design change.[466] Any number of theories could be drawn from the evolution of shields in conjunction with the developments and introduction of new offensive weaponry. However likely, there is a lack of definitive evidence with regard to the matter, rendering absolute conclusions practically impossible to gain. Without the discovery of new physical evidence, the best way to draw any more specific conclusions is to carry out experimental archaeology with reconstructed ancient Egyptian weapons and shields.

Personal Protection: Helmets

Moving on from the shields, there are several other aspects of ancient Egyptian defence that should be examined. Another key piece of defensive equipment in any society is the helmet and there are several variations of protective headwear that the ancient Egyptians used in combat. As with the shields, there is little-to-no surviving artefactual evidence for helmets, so a great deal of the information we have on them comes from pictorial evidence.

For much of Dynastic Egyptian history, the evidence seems to suggest the soldiers wore no protective headwear; indeed, the first known appearance of any sort of helmet being used by soldiers occurs during the New Kingdom.[467] One of the most popular, if somewhat unusual, current theories is that before the advent of helmets, ancient Egyptian soldiers used a rather ingenious method of wearing their hair in a thick, bushy style as a way of protecting their heads from injury.[468] Contemporary artistic depictions (such as the models of the spearmen found in Mehseti's tomb) and the preserved remains of the soldiers from the mass burial near the mortuary temple of Montu-hotep II at Deir el-Bahri seem to support this argument.[469] These soldiers wore their ample, thick hair tightly-curled,[470] a style that could possibly have helped to protect their skulls. It is not known for certain whether or not this hair-style worn by the soldiers would actually have saved lives but Stonborough has reasonably suggested that a suitably designed set of archaeological experiments could be used to gain some answers.[471]

None-too-surprisingly a theory that supports the use of tightly braided hair as a form of defence has its critics. If you look at the shape of the helmets represented at Saqqara and Medinet Habu you can see a distinct similarity to the hairstyles that were depicted on soldiers and labourers throughout the dynastic period, particularly

Figure 3.7

in the shape they take around the ears and the forehead[472] **(Figure 3.7)**. Stonborough theorises that past archaeologists may mistakenly have interpreted images of helmets as being coiled hair instead; this is something that could have occurred with relative ease, especially if depictions of helmets in other portrayals/reliefs had less pronounced domes than those shown in the Saqqara images.[473]

Voices along this line are an exciting addition to the study of pre-New Kingdom helmets, as it could potentially be that helmets were used more widely in ancient Egypt than previously thought.[474] However, without further comparative study of the several and varied depictions of soldiers in some form of armour/defensive equipment found at ancient Egyptian sites, it is impossible to say which of these theories is correct.

The predominant current theory suggests that the New Kingdom saw the advent of Egyptian soldiers wearing helmets in combat. At this time there was a rise in artistic portrayals of helmets being used, examples of which can be seen in the battle scenes against the Sea Peoples at Medinet Habu and a series of paintings and reliefs at Saqqara which depicts helmets alongside other types of military equipment[475] **(Figure 3.8)**. There are currently no examples of a surviving Egyptian helmet that have been found, although there is a possible model that exists in the form of a funerary headdress composed of faience that is held in the Metropolitan Museum.[476] This artefact is no doubt interesting but, as with other ceremonial items, there are several issues which cause difficulty when trying to draw conclusions from it about ancient Egyptian helmets used in combat. It has apparently been dated to the Twenty-Sixth Dynasty (and therefore it is possibly not a native Egyptian design) and there is nothing to suggest that the model was meant to signify a military helmet. On the contrary, there are no depictions of this style of helmet ever being worn by any Egyptian soldiers.[477]

This rather comprehensive lack of evidence does make it a little tricky to make too many suppositions about the exact nature of the form these helmets took. It has been assumed by some that the helmets depicted at Saqqara were composed of bronze with some sort of cloth base (perhaps added in order to make the bronze helmet more comfortable... in relative terms!).[478] It is indeed probable that a helmet made from a hard material such as bronze would have had been worn with some form of softer material on the inside to protect the head (to help absorb shocks and prevent chafing). However there is no firm evidence to support any suggestion that the Saqqara images do in fact portray bronze helmets.[479] Stonborough points

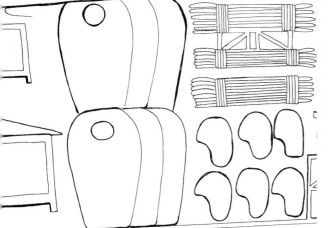

Figure 3.8

out that none of the images available are detailed enough to allow for a researcher to make a completely certain classification of the materials New Kingdom helmets were made from. Indeed, he even queries whether the lack of artefactual evidence may not suggest that they were composed of more perishable materials, such as rawhide (like the shields) or possibly even plant materials.[480] Helmets made from animal materials were certainly known in Egypt. Whilst acknowledging the rarity of helmets in ancient Egypt, Shaw highlights that a version became part of royal regalia in the New Kingdom, taking the form of a war helmet of stitched leather complete with leather discs sewn onto it.[481] There are doubts as to whether or not this is actually an effective form of a defensive helmet but it is interesting nevertheless. This has definite implications for future archaeological study and has significant potential for more experimental archaeology.

Shaw goes no further into detail regarding alternative types of helmet other than briefly mentioning the strange helmets apparently worn by the Sherden mercenaries as seen in Kadesh battle reliefs at Abu Simbel: a rounded leather/rawhide helmet complete with curving horns either side of the helmet and a spike coming out of the central top; and in case all of that was not enough, there also appears to be a sphere or disc perched on top of the central spike[482] **(Figure 3.9).** This odd fusion of ancient Egyptian and clichéd Viking seems a little out of place in relation to the stylistic conventions of Dynastic Egyptian military style, so perhaps this can be explained away by the fact that these were apparently only worn by mercenaries and not by full-time ancient Egyptian soldiers. (Whether or not the Sherdan mercenaries' enemies were defeated by laughing so much at the helmets that they were unable to put up much of a fight is not mentioned).

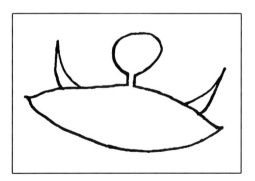 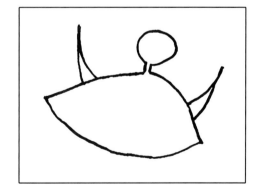

Figure 3.9

Personal Protection: Body Armour

Aside from shields and helmets, one other aspect of defence available for ancient Egyptian soldiers was a form of body armour. Some scholars claim that before the advent of the New Kingdom no body armour was worn by ancient Egyptian soldiers.[483] Over time bands wrapped around their chests began to appear, followed by linen bindings until more conventional armour, scale armour and corselets, arrived on the scene.

Hayes supports the idea that there was no early use of body armour and highlights that the first addition to a soldier's wardrobe came in the Middle Kingdom. Around this time artistic evidence arises showing the occasional use of straps or bands that crossed the chest, though unfortunately there is no mention of what material these bands may have been composed of.[484] As no physical bands remain we cannot know for certain what they were made of, however some scholars suggested linen or cured skin, as the material used would have to have been flexible enough to wrap around a torso.[485]

The bands are generally portrayed as being very narrow strips, which hardly cover any of the most vulnerable areas of the soldiers' bodies, such as the belly, the neck, or even the kidneys. It is hard to believe that these narrow strips could have provided an effective defence against most sharp-force bladed weapons (such as swords or axes) and certainly not against any blunt-force weapons (such as maces or clubs).[486] It would not be remarkable to expect that if these bands were actually proper pieces of defensive equipment, they would be represented widely on ancient Egyptian soldiers. However, they are actually portrayed in a somewhat haphazard fashion in ancient Egyptian artwork; with archers being portrayed wearing these bands slightly more frequently than other troop types.[487] One thing that is very interesting to note is that there is absolutely no trace of any straps or bands worn across the chest on any of the wooden spearmen or archers from the tomb of Mehseti[488] **(see Figure 3.3)**.

A logical theory that could be applied to these straps/bands is that they were not pieces of defensive equipment but were, in fact, a way of carrying certain items. It has been pointed out that the straps were used by sailors and dancers as well as soldiers, suggesting that they were perhaps mostly used as a carrying device with any defensive aspect being a secondary result.[489] This is particularly pertinent when you realise that the soldiers of the time wore linen kilts that do not appear to have had pockets, meaning that an alternative form of carrying excess items (such as secondary or tertiary weapons, or small personal items) would need to have been used.[490] The straps/bands/bindings seen on some artistic portrayals would have been perfect for transporting these other items. This could either be done by direct attachment (almost like a bandoleer) or perhaps via the addition of a small bag, something that makes sense, particularly when you consider that these straps are depicted a little more frequently on archers.[491] The archers would certainly have needed to transport extra items, such as spare strings, arm braces and other materials for the upkeep and use of the bows, along with their arrows. This is supported by what was found in a surviving kitbag of an Egyptian archer. As they had more need for this extra storage, it would make sense for the archers to be shown wearing these bands/straps more frequently than other troops.[492]

There are a couple of examples where the bands crossing the torso were seemingly used to secure a plate to the chest, quite possibly for defensive purposes, in what could be one of the first examples of a proper breastplate[493] **(Figure 3.10)**. However, as Stonborough points out, the soldiers shown wearing these 'breastplates' are not shown actively fighting, but seem to be participating in a procession.[494] His theory is that these breastplates were not designed for use in battle, but instead held a symbolic significance and would only be worn on ceremonial occasions. They may have been the symbol of a certain rank or position as well, rather than simply being a functional piece of armour.[495]

Before the advent of more recognisable hide/leather/metal armour, linen wrappings and bindings were used to defend ancient Egyptian soldiers. These bindings appeared from the New Kingdom onwards and are argued by Stonborough and McDermott to be probably defensive in nature. This can be backed-up by the fact that such bindings are used even today by some African tribes' warriors as protection against blows from weaponry.[496] When the bindings are shown in ancient Egyptian art, they seem to be designed to cover the entire torso of the soldiers, reaching up around the shoulders as well and are particularly associated with acts of warfare when worn by Pharaohs in the famous smiting scenes.[497]

The effectiveness of these linen bindings has been demonstrated by experimental archaeology which confirmed that tightly wrapped linen bindings could resist blows that were delivered with even modern sharpened-steel blades.[498] Whilst these linen bindings certainly would not have completely prevented injury from a sharp-force weapon (with the wearer possibly suffering even a severe wound), it is suggested that they would have moderated the effects and severity of such an injury.[499] This is probably why, in conjunction with the sheer lightness of such a material, linen was used in this way as bindings and again why it was used to some extent in the manufacture of some of the later, more complex forms of body armour in the New Kingdom.[500]

The New Kingdom saw the advent of corselets, which began to regularly appear in portrayals of Pharaohs and deities as apparel that covered the abdomen and fastened over the Pharaoh's shoulder via the use of two straps.[501] According to Stonborough, these corselets were often shown as being covered in colourful scales, perhaps as a precursor to the more practical leather scale armour that arrived later on.[502] One of the more well-known examples of such a corselet comes, of course, from the tomb of Tutankhamun. It is described as being an ostentatious item, set in gold and composed of coloured glass and semi-precious gems.[503] Stonborough makes that assumption that this piece of armour was never intended to be functional and was votive in design. This is not improbable as it is unlikely that anyone would want to risk damaging such a beautiful (and expensive) piece of work (although the Pharaohs did like to show-off quite a bit in general!).[504] Perhaps Tutankhamun wore this item for ceremonial purposes – maybe for a military parade when he would want to look as impressive and god-like as possible for his troops.

The jewelled scales seen on Tutankhamun's corselet could well be a decorative and ritualistic take on the functional armour of a soldier. It is possible that the scales covering the corselets shown on the New Kingdom depictions of deities and Pharaohs may have taken inspiration from the introduction of the more functional

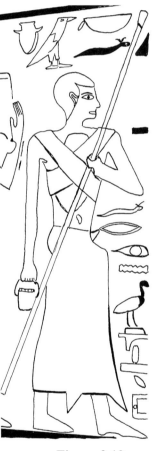

piece of armour into Egypt: Scale Armour.[505] Scale armour featured a great deal in ancient Near Eastern warfare but does not seem to have been a part of ancient Egyptian warfare until the Second Intermediate Period at the earliest.[506] The general opinion seems to be that scale armour was introduced along with the chariot and composite bow by the Hyksos during this period; in fact, it would seem that New Kingdom Egypt owes a great deal of their technological advances in warfare to the Hyksos.[507]

On examination of both artistic representations and artefactual evidence, Stonborough suggests that these 'suits' of scale armour were long garments that covered the chest, the shoulders, the abdomen, and possibly the thighs of the wearer (depending on their height), and comprised rows of scales (of either metal or rawhide) which were laced onto padded linen.[508] Once again we must look to the marvellous collection from the tomb of Tutankhamun for one of the best pieces of artefactual evidence. It is relatively unusual, in that the armour is made from rawhide scales and is in such impressive condition; this is a rare occurrence as the majority of such finds are bronze scales, either found individually or in small groups.[509] One of these bronze scales was found in a coppersmith's hoard at el-Lisht, with another example (a group of bronze scales) being found at the palace of Malkata belonging to Amenhotep III.[510] But these scales have always been found in very small numbers, with all the scales found across the Middle East not even being enough

Figure 3.10

to make a full piece of scale armour.[511] It has been suggested that these 'suits' of armour were not really thrown away once they had sustained some damage because of the functional and economical value that they held. This, on top of the ease with which such bronze scales could be melted down for reuse and the likelihood of linen and rawhide decaying, is possibly why so few examples of such pieces of armour survive in the archaeological record.[512]

How commonly scale armour was used by the New Kingdom military is unclear – as with other items of armour and defensive equipment, the scale armour can be hard to identify in artistic depictions from the period.   There are a few examples which are possible images of scale armour (such as the Egyptian soldiers depicted fighting the Sea Peoples on boats in the battle scenes at Medinet Habu), but nothing can be seen with any degree of certainty.[513] It has been suggested that the scale armour was in fact used mostly by charioteers, perhaps forming part of a package of military equipment that included armour, chariot, and bow.[514] Whichever soldiers wore such armour, the proficiency of this type of defensive equipment was displayed by some brilliant archaeological experiments carried out by Hulit and Richardson,[515] who tested the armour against replica New Kingdom era weaponry: archery equipment and bronze axes. These experiments included the testing of three different variations of scale armour: a piece of armour composed of bronze scales, one made of rawhide scales, and one that was a combination of the two.[516]

The results from these experiments were fascinating; the armour held up very well against the bronze-tipped arrow, with the interesting observation that the armour comprising of the alternating bronze and rawhide scales seemed to provide an almost perfect balance between weight and protection. This combination armour apparently deflected the arrows just as well as the armour that was made entirely of bronze scales, with the added bonus of being lighter (and therefore much easier to wear, with potentially more scope for manoeuvrability).[517] The bronze-scale armour was also tested by having a replica New Kingdom axe used against it; the result being that whilst the axe did not, for the most part, pierce the surface, it did inflict substantial damage: the strings that attached the bronze scales to each other and to the linen backing were cut with whole rows of bronze scales falling off the armour.[518] Whilst this may suggest that the scale armour was more vulnerable to an axe attack, the damage could have been caused by the scales of the replica surface not being attached together with sufficient tightness, allowing the blade of the axe to reach the bindings. It is also possible that the material used for the binding and backing of the scales was inadequate for the job it was meant to do, contributing to the ease with which the axe blade could have caused such damage.[519] Whatever damage the scale armour sustained from an axe blade, the protection they potentially offered from arrow-fire made them vital to the soldiers who wore them on the open battlefield,[520] something that would particularly be useful for a charioteer.

Experimental archaeology of this type can prove to be invaluable to archaeologists. Naturally at times it can produce more questions than answers and at other times can completely throw-off what had been previously thought to be a fascinating and plausible hypothesis. Two such interesting examples of experimental archaeology in relation to both offensive and defensive warfare will be discussed in Chapter 5.

As we have seen, the methods of defence used by the ancient Egyptian military varied a great deal throughout the Dynastic Period. Although there is some evidence of public protection, through the building of fortresses at strategic locations in ancient Egyptian-controlled land, there are questions as to how effective these fortresses really were. For instance, how much of their effectiveness was down to their imposing nature? Did they even pay a particularly crucial role in the defence of Egypt's borders? They certainly did not seem to be used in offensive warfare as much as they were to defend against invasions and infiltrations and to protect valuable trade routes.

Most of the information available is around the personal defence equipment of Egypt's troops. There is certainly evidence for the use of helmets and some forms of body armour, both in artefactual and artistic evidence. One of the most interesting pieces of this defence equipment, however, was the shield. The ancient Egyptian shield was an item of deceptive simplicity, remarkable flexibility, and impressive defensive capabilities. This was of particular interest in the series of experiments carried out at the University of York in 2011, which will be looked at in detail in Chapter 5.

What we can take away from looking at ancient Egypt's defensive capabilities, is that they were impressive for such an ancient civilisation with what could be seen as relative limited military resources and technology, particularly in the earlier days of the Dynastic Period. During the Old and Middle Kingdoms there was no access to the kind of technology that was used by other later civilisations (e.g. Classical Greek and Roman, Medieval), when personal defence was improved by more developed technologies and armour design. Of course, these later periods saw warfare on a larger scale than had previously occurred with the rise of Alexander the Great, the Persian Empire and the Roman Empire.

Hopefully we now have a more firm understanding of the nature of warfare in Ancient Egypt, as well as the range of weapons used during this period. As we have seen, the military was predominantly masculine in its make up, but we are now to move on to those shadowy figures who occasionally became involved in warfare (either through choice or unfortunate circumstance): Women.

4

Women and Warfare in Ancient Egypt

There is one very interesting aspect of ancient Egyptian warfare that is studied rarely, despite how fascinating it is: the extent to which women were part of the Egyptian military. It is particularly noticeable that previous works covering Egyptian warfare fail to make any mention of women in a military context. Nevertheless, together with the position of women within Egyptian society as a whole, the roles of New Kingdom female monarchs such as Ahhotep, Hatshepsut, Nefertiti, and Tawosret (to name but a few) need to be scrutinized far more closely given the apparent warrior-like sensibilities of earlier women rulers such as Nitocris of the Old Kingdom. If women could hold positions of political power, it is a possibility that some may also have held positions of military power; it is certainly no coincidence that one of the most important deities in ancient Egyptian religion was Sekhmet, the female goddess of warfare. It is also apparent that some of the highest offices of state normally held by men could also be held by women.[521] It is certainly worth having at least a brief look at some of the examples of women being involved in warfare.

When studying the involvement of women in ancient Egyptian warfare, certain Predynastic female weapons burials are a key part of this argument. The fact that women were buried with maces from such as early period cannot simply be dismissed as evidence of votive deposits, with burials such as grave 1488 at Naqada (on the west bank of the Nile) revealing that women could buried with functional weapons. The burial is definitely that of a female and it contained two mace-heads: one piriform mace-head of alabaster and one conical mace-head of syenite,[522] with no suggestion that either weapon was a votive object. Similarly, Predynastic Naqada grave 1401 contained the body of an adult female accompanied by three stone mace-heads and a flint knife.[523] These women could well have been important within Naqada society, indicated by the fact that they were buried with functional rather than votive weapons.

In further excavations at the Predynastic site of Naqada, some other female burials included mace heads as part of the grave goods.[524] This brief mention of a Predynastic site is relevant to this book as it demonstrates the early appearance of the mace, the weapon that went on to become such a significant part of Dynastic Egyptian iconography. Naqada burial 1401 held the body of an adult female and the remains of up to six children, interred with no less than three stone mace-heads and a flint knife.[525] Another significant female burial at the same site is 1417.[526] This grave is particularly important as it contained flint knives and a painted limestone conical mace-head together with an ivory comb, a bone comb, a bird top, and a Hathor head top.[527] It is possible to hypothesize on the basis of these burial goods that 1417 was the burial of a woman with some degree of importance within Predynastic Naqada society, the mace-head buried with her possibly serving at least a partly votive purpose as it is so highly decorated.

Yet another female burial at Naqada in which the mace-heads were unlikely to have been votive is grave 1488. There is no hesitation in stating that the burial is definitely that of a woman, although there is no indication of her age.[528] Her burial contained two mace-heads: one piriform mace-head of alabaster (which was placed in front of the forehead of the deceased) and one conical mace-head of syenite (which was found placed behind the back of the body).[529] Not only was this particular woman buried with two mace-heads but neither weapon appeared to be votive. Plenty of examples of clay, wood, or ivory (and therefore ritual) mace-heads were found in such burials, but in grave 1488 the two mace-heads were certainly potentially functional, even if it is impossible to prove they were used as such by this particular woman. Even if the weapons were proven to be symbolic rather than functional, what we learned (in the previous chapter) about maces and what they represent highlights that these maces would certainly be an indication of some level of power held by this woman, whoever she was.

In analysis of such burials of the pre-unification period, it has been concluded that some of the tombs belonging to women were larger than those provided for male remains. This would suggest that in these centres the women may well have been community leaders, as generally the largest graves in these cemeteries were reserved for rulers.[530] This is a significant observation since traditionally-known rulers in Egyptian history had larger tombs than their subjects.[531] Although these women would not have held sole power as pharaoh at this time (Egypt not yet being unified, instead of being divided into several smaller 'states' or nomarchs), they may have been rulers of their local area. Women can clearly be seen in some position of power before the unification and subsequent Dynastic period. These women could also have been the widows of the men who held power in the area before their death. These female burials are also contemporaneous with those female Predynastic burials containing mace-heads discussed above, both suggesting that women had some political or military importance within their societies. If this was indeed the case, the notion of a female leader would not have been new to the Egyptians and if a woman could hold a position of power in Predynastic times, they may also have held comparable status in Dynastic times.

One of the most famous occurrences of women involved in warfare was discussed by William Flinders Petrie in his 1898 work, *Deshasheh* (**Figure 4.1**). In an image that provides arguably clear evidence that Egyptian women could be involved in combat in some form, the east wall of the Fourth Dynasty tomb of Anta at Deshasheh "reveals epigraphic evidence for women fighting to defend a town":[532] the women of the town of Sati fighting off Egyptian and Bedawi invaders.[533] In the uppermost register of the scene, a Sati woman stabs the chest of an invading Bedawi who had made his way up a siege ladder into the town enclosure and a second woman, accompanied by a child, has forced a Bedawi to surrender and break his bow.[534]

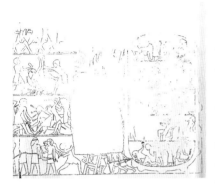

Figure 4.1

In the next register down, the chief of the settlement is seemingly tearing his hair out in distress whilst one of the townswomen is forcing back an invading soldier who is trying to make his way into the enclosure.[535] So as the male leader apparently bemoans his sorry fate, it is left to the women to defend their town. The middle scene in the third row down depicts two groups of two women each bringing down an invader, whilst the fourth register features another Sati woman who has overpowered a Bedawi and pulled him over by his armpits.[536] The fifth and final row of the wall scene portrays two men and one woman who seem to be listening for enemy sappers mining the bases of the walls of the town enclosure, whilst there is the dead, or at the very least unconscious, body of one of the invaders.[537] It has therefore been suggested that these striking scenes "show that women could engage in combat if necessary, and could be reasonably adept both with and without the aid of weaponry".[538] So although women did not necessarily take part in combat or warfare on a regular basis, there is evidence that they did so at least occasionally.

Nor is the Deshasheh tomb scene an isolated example, there is evidence for a female guard buried in the Sixth Dynasty necropolis of Teti at Saqqara.[539] With three women granted their own tombs in this cemetery, the third has particular relevance for this study. Known by three names (Merinebti, Merinebti-ankhteti and Semut), she also bore several titles, including that of 'acquaintance of the king' and 'tenant landholder'; the role of a 'tenant landholder' usually responsible for the provisioning of the palace or temple.[540] However, this title, *ḫntj-š*, traditionally translated as 'tenant', has more recently been translated as employee or attendant.[541] It has been pointed out that this title is held by those who are described as providing protection for the king and when portrayed they are carrying batons and are responsible for carrying out the tasks of a guard or bodyguard.[542] In the case of Merinebti the term *ḫntj-š* does not have the feminine determinative *t*, with the hieroglyphic text simply translating as 'guard', so it has been determined that the title held by Merinebti was that of 'female guard'.[543]

The exact duties and responsibilities of the female holders of this title are unfortunately unclear and, although there is some suggestion that they may have served in the most restricted parts of the royal harem, this theory, is purely speculative. In general, guards did not have individual tombs,[544] so this woman presumably held a position of some power to have been granted her own tomb in the royal cemetery. So far, this is the only occurrence of a 'female guard' having an independent tomb but it is possible that further evidence may be found in the future.[545] Whilst there is absolutely no evidence to suggest that this woman took part in active combat, it is interesting that she was granted what could be seen as a quasi-military title. Further research into what sort of role this would have been, and if there were any more examples of female guards, would be beneficial to the discipline.

There are several examples of female weapons burials in the Dynastic Period as well as those seen in Predynastic cemeteries. The Twelfth Dynasty burial of Senebtisi at Lisht contained an array of weaponry, including an alabaster piriform mace with a gold-mounted wooden shaft.[546] Hayes admits that it would have been possible for this mace to have been actively used as a weapon, even though this has yet to be proven.[547] The same burial also contained a conical rock crystal mace head,[548] an unusual choice of material which would also benefit from experimental archaeology at some point in the future to test its durability as a possible weapon.

Another significant Twelfth Dynasty interment, discovered within the pyramid of Amenemhat III at Dashur, is that of two middle-aged queens from the reign of this king. Both were buried with granite and alabaster mace-heads, along with jewellery and perfume pots;[549] their mace-heads, like the ones found in Senebtisi's burial, could possibly have been used as functional weapons although this has not yet been proven.

Another Dynastic weapons burial, this time dated to the end of the Second Intermediate Period, provides one very important example of powerful ancient Egyptian woman who also happened to have some involvement with warfare. Queen Ahhotep, of the late Seventeenth Dynasty, was possibly the wife of the Pharaoh Seqenenre Tao II.[550] After Seqenenre was killed in combat, Ahhotep was said to have led troops into battle and was rewarded for her valour. Whilst not a reigning pharaoh, Queen Ahhotep is a highly significant figure in the events of this period. The burial goods found in her tomb included a considerable quantity of weaponry and there is sufficient evidence to suggest that Ahhotep was actively engaged in the planning of military engagements, if not in the leading of troops. It is certainly possible that the queen went into battle herself: the Karnak Stela is very direct in its description of Ahhotep, claiming that this queen cared for the soldiers, bringing back fugitives, and gathering the country's deserters, all on top of pacifying Egypt and expelling rebels to boot.[551] Ahhotep supposedly rallied her soldiers to continue fighting the enemy when her first-born son, Kamose, fell in battle, which apparently led the way to the re-unification of Egypt.[552]

There is some confusion between archaeologists as to the number of queens named Ahhotep, with conflicting accounts of the burials associated with this name and few surviving records relating to them.[553] At least one Ahhotep had significant amounts of weaponry buried with her; this Ahhotep is likely to have been the queen described on the stela set up at Karnak temple. This woman could have been Seqenenre's wife or she could have been the wife of Kamose. There has certainly been some debate over the last century as to whether or not Ahhotep I and Ahhotep II are in fact the same woman.

Whether there was one Ahhotep or two, the weapons found in one of their tombs are highly significant. She was buried with three daggers and thirteen axes bearing both the names of Ahmose I and his elder brother Kamose[554] (**Figure 4.2**). The names of Ahmose I and Kamose being inscribed on the weapons is hugely significant, as highly decorated ceremonial axes that bore the name of the reigning pharaoh were usually presented as honours for courage in battle[555] (**Figure 4.3**). Yet again, Ahhotep's involvement in active combat is emphasised by her burial goods; these ceremonial axes are just as telling as the three Golden Flies of Valour she was buried with. At a time when sickle swords were adapting to the developing armour technology, axes were also converted to types that were better suited to piercing attacks, two of the best examples of these were found in Queen Ahhotep's burial.[556] Both these axes were short, with wide edges which would provide a firm blow that would certainly cause a large and potentially debilitating cut.[557] These two axes of Ahhotep are excellent indicators of changing weapons technology during this early New Kingdom period.

The weapons, which also included a javelin head and an archer's brace, could be construed as purely votive

Figure 4.2

objects. However, their discovery alongside the 'Golden Flies of Valour' military decorations emphasises the militaristic attribute of the grave goods buried with Queen Ahhotep, particularly as the Flies were only awarded to someone who had

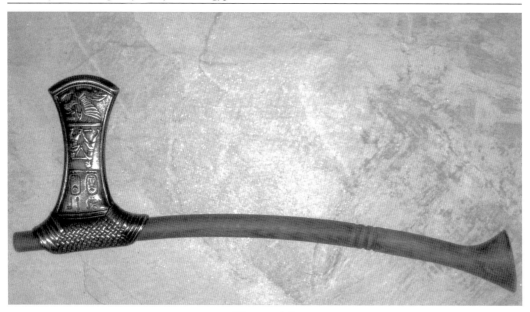

Figure 4.3

personally excelled in battle.[558] The actions of Ahhotep described in the Karnak stele (leading soldiers victoriously into battle) would justify her right to be buried with such awards. While Ahhotep is a critically important figure in the examination of women associated with weapons in ancient Egypt, the Eighteenth Dynasty itself is a time of Egyptian history that is full of formidable women.[559] It could also be said that the Eighteenth Dynasty was a Dynasty of formidable males, with pharaohs such as Amenhotep II and Thutmose III. However, the fact that there were so many examples of 'formidable women' in the Eighteenth Dynasty, compared to some of the other Dynasties, does highlight the importance of the Eighteenth Dynasty in the study of women, power, and warfare in ancient Egypt.

The best known of Egypt's female pharaohs is the Eighteenth Dynasty Hatshepsut. With widespread evidence for her reign she is obviously an extremely significant figure in this study. Although she officially came to the throne as regent for her young stepson (after the death of her husband Thutmose II) it is possible that Hatshepsut took on some pharaonic duties during the reign of her husband, before she became regent, due to her husband's suggested illness.[560] According to Callender, in a critical examination of Hatshepsut's reign, this is something Queen Ahhotep had done for her son Ahmose on a regular basis; so whilst Hatshepsut undertaking duties for her husband may not have been the most unusual of occurrences, it would have proven her capabilities and perhaps given her a taste for power.[561]

Whilst Hatshepsut initially became regent for her stepson, she then took the role of reigning pharaoh for herself (c. 1479 BC). She apparently did not give up her regency at the agreed time and attempted to establish her own legitimacy as pharaoh by discrediting her husband's reign and claiming that her father, Thutmose I, had presented her to his court as his chosen heiress to his throne.[562] It seems highly likely that Hatshepsut would have been aware of the Second Dynasty edict that stated that a woman might legitimately rule Egypt as pharaoh. There had been at least two female pharaohs before her, suggesting that her biological sex was no great impediment to her rule.[563] Though this bid for power displays Hatshepsut's intelligence and ambition, her reign also demonstrates some military expertise, particularly as she conducted (or at least ordered) five different military campaigns during her time as pharaoh.[564]

Initially some scholars believed that Hatshepsut carried out no military campaigns during her reign, comparing her unfavourably with her successor Thutmose III. They describe Hatshepsut as never having any military campaigns or conquests, whilst Thutmose III apparently became a great conqueror.[565] Several works in the middle of the Twentieth Century follow the traditionally-held view that Hatshepsut was more of a builder than a fighter, who concentrated solely on internal development (building works and commercial developments etc.) as well as peaceful endeavours.[566]

Although this long-held opinion was proven to be incorrect by a 1960s publication, discussing the five military campaigns organised by Hatshepsut,[567] the erroneous views of the academic work of the 1950s was repeated by others even after Redford's work was published. Work done in the late 1960s suggests that Hatshepsut was simply not interested in warfare. They even went so far as to suggest that, having been brought up in a military atmosphere in her father's court and then being married to a military man, she'd had enough of it.[568] Hatshepsut's achievements are also dismissed by claiming that she had no part in them, that she enjoyed a peaceful reign only because the pharaohs before her had fought for it.[569] Certainly, the work done in the 1960s[570] would seem to disprove this idea that Hatshepsut had no interest in military campaigns.

Examples of evidence for the military campaigns organised by Hatshepsut are taken from the island of Sehēl. The first example involves two limestone blocks found at Karnak, dated to Hatshepsut's reign, which describes her as being a protectress of her people, having the Asiatics in fear of her, and keeping the land of Nubia submissive to the pharaoh.[571] This inscription refers to a military campaign of Hatshepsut, with the reference to the fearful Asiatic peoples potentially referring to a policy of active warfare instead of the commercial goals suggested by other contemporary scholars.[572]

More comprehensive evidence of military campaigns during Hatshepsut's reign comes from her funerary temple at Deir el-Bahri, where a description of a campaign into Nubia states that the defeat of the Nubians was comprehensive, recounting the number of dead as being so large that the exact numbers are unknown, with all foreign lands turning back from war with Hatshepsut on account of her greatness.[573] Another reference to Hatshepsut's military campaigns at Deir el-Bahri is one part of a text, apparently corroborated by an official who fought in a campaign in the Sinai during Hatshepsut's co-regency with Thutmose III, describing Hatshepsut's arrow amid the Northerners, suggesting that Hatshpsut was personally involved in the battle against the Asiatics.[574]

One of the most convincing pieces of evidence for Hatshepsut's involvement in military campaigns comes from Sehēl again. This evidence takes the form of a rock inscription written by Hatshepsut's royal treasurer, in which he describes the king Ka-(ma)-re overthrowing Nubians, taking their chiefs prisoner, and destroying the land of Nubia.[575] As the 'king' is named as Maat-kare (Ka-(ma)-re), this is a very significant piece of text, as Maat-kare was the throne name of Hatshepsut. The passage refers to the king as 'he' but it is important to realise that Hatshepsut alternated between referring to herself as 'she' and 'he' in official inscriptions. In this case, the military nature of this passage apparently called for the use of the masculine pronoun.[576] As this text shows, masculine pronouns were used for women in military contexts, so it is possible argue that other documentary records will not unambiguously demonstrate the use of feminine pronouns for women going into battle. This may explain what some scholars argue is a *lack* of women in a military context in the historical record; it could be that they were simply represented in textual sources by the use of male pronouns. This text is also important because it shows Hatshepsut to have been leading campaigns herself, taking an active role in warfare and military campaigns. Of course, this may simply be exaggeration on the part of Hatshepsut overstating her bravado before her subjects. Yet the same may be said about any of Egypt's pharaohs, male or female, who proclaimed to the world their prowess in battle and success in war, a good example being Ramesses II and his version of the Battle of Kadesh when compared to the example of his Hittite opponents – an exercise in blatant embellishment and hyperbole.

Another account which suggests that Hatshepsut ran military campaigns during her reign is a tomb inscription from Dra Abu el-Naga, near Deir el-Bahri. Written by a scribe called Djehuty, the inscription refers to the booty collected (by a female ruler) from the Kushites, who are described as being both vile and cowards. This inscription seems to prove that Hatshepsut led her troops into battle on at least one occasion against Nubia, as the inscription suggests that Hatshepsut herself took the 'booty' from the defeated Nubians.[577] Whilst it is possible that this was indeed the case, it may also be possible that this is merely a fictional account designed to create a particular image for a female pharaoh trying to display her power and might. Yet on the other hand, why would a scribe feel the need to be creative with the truth on his own monument, unless perhaps he wanted to curry favour with his pharaoh by portraying her as a great leader of armies.

Hatshepsut can often be seen in the archaeological record holding weaponry. One Eighteenth Dynasty depiction of Hatshepsut, before she became Pharaoh, is found on an obelisk from Abu Tig and forms the lowest register of figures.[578] The queen (as she was then) appears on each side of the obelisk wearing a tunic and carrying a mace.[579] Although this is not a smiting scene, the mace is still a hugely important symbol of power. Therefore it is vital that it is recognised that Hatshepsut was notable and influential even before becoming Pharaoh. Another scene showing Hatshepsut carrying a mace was carved when she was Pharaoh and is found on the north obelisk at Karnak,[580] again emphasising Hatshepsut's power and importance (**Figure 4.4**).

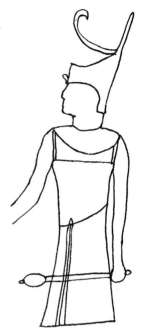

Figure 4.4

Furthermore, Hatshepsut's daughter Neferure is also depicted with a mace when still a princess in scenes in her mother's funerary temple at Deir el-Bahari.[581] Here, the young girl is portrayed with the side-lock of hair, denoting her youthful status, and she carries a mace. This is in contrast to Neferure's portraits once she had taken on the role of queen to accompany her mother as king when, instead of a mace, Neferure is depicted holding a sceptre intended to denote her status as queen.[582] The use of the mace in these images only emphasises the potential future power of Neferure, adding weight to the theory that Hatshepsut was intending to have Neferure succeed her as pharaoh after her death.[583]

Perhaps one of the more controversial examples of a female pharaoh displaying warrior-like qualities is Nefertiti. Nefertiti, portrayed in the guise of a reigning monarch, stands on the royal barge and wields a *khopesh* against a female foreign prisoner in what can only be described as a typical 'smiting scene'[584] (**Figure 4.5**).

As the 'smiting scene' motif was traditionally limited to a reigning pharaoh, it is most revealing that Nefertiti was depicted in this way and is another piece of evidence supporting the theory that Nefertiti reigned as pharaoh, certainly as co-regent with her husband, and possibly, after his death, as sole ruler.

Samson also mentions this smiting scene, from a limestone block found at Amarna, believing that it indicates Nefertiti's pharaonic power.[585] In this scene, Nefertiti takes the role of the pharaonic 'warrior', wearing her

Figure 4.5

instantly recognisable blue crown and stripped to the waist, wearing the ceremonial traditionally male-style kilt of a pharaoh. This corresponds to the act that she is about to carry out, an act traditionally the domain of the pharaoh.[586] As Samson agrees, Nefertiti was generally depicted in her ways and dress as being principally feminine apart from when she was portrayed in this scene so seemingly symbolic of her pharaonic power.[587] As discussed earlier, smiting scenes were expressions of power and were especially important at times of unification; a pharaoh wishing to display strength and authority would be depicted in a smiting pose to display dominance, so it is extremely interesting that Nefertiti herself is portrayed in such a scene, suggesting she was a reigning monarch in her own right.[588] In addition, although women were rarely shown driving their own chariots, Nefertiti is apparently shown driving her own vehicle and in charge of her own horses.[589]

It has already been stated that Nefertiti is portrayed driving her own chariot in tomb scenes at Amarna.[590] In such scenes she wields a whip to encourage her horses to speed up. It seems unlikely that there was a completely insurmountable barrier preventing a woman from being able to physically drive a relatively light Egyptian chariot. It may not have happened on a regular basis (although there is nothing to suggest it did not) but it is represented in art, with examples of Nefertiti driving a chariot by herself, as seen in the tomb of Merya.[591] The light design and extensive use of binding in chariot assembly also meant that they could be constructed, dismantled, rebuilt, and repaired very easily, which could have been crucial in battle.

The final female pharaoh briefly examined here is Tawosret (Tauseret, Tewosret), who reigned as pharaoh at the end of the Nineteenth Dynasty under the throne name Sit-Re.[592] Although evidence for the reign of Tawosret appears in the ancient king lists and she is mentioned by Manetho,[593] she is rarely mentioned in standard text books such as Shaw and Nicholson's *British Museum Dictionary of Ancient Egypt*.[594] Tawosret's kingship could have been presented in such a way as to suggest a Dynastic Egyptian concept of an equal balance between the masculine and feminine.[595] Tawosret adopted the traditionally masculine blue helmet in her portrayals but ensured her nomen and prenomen underlined her status as a female pharaoh: she is named as the daughter of Ra and the Lady of Ta-merit.[596] This fits in well with the ancient Egyptian concept of gender duality.

As the last legitimate member of the royal dynastic family of the Nineteenth Dynasty,[597] Gardiner describes Tawosret as one of only four women in Dynastic Egypt who took on the role of Pharaoh.[598] For all his reluctance to acknowledge female pharaohs, Gardiner does admit that Tawosret is of vital importance in the Nineteenth Dynasty; Tawosret was the only 'queen' of the Nineteenth Dynasty to have a tomb based in the Valley of the Kings and the only 'queen' to have built her own temple.[599] Even Gardiner is willing to admit that Tawosret wielded her power as a definite pharaoh not 'just' a queen.[600]

Figure 4.6

It is most likely Tawosret who is depicted on a Nineteenth Dynasty ostracon sketch firing arrows from a moving chariot in battle **(Figure 4.6)**; her pharaonic status symbolised by the uraeus (quite clearly and deliberately drawn on an otherwise sketchy illustration) is shown on her brow as she rides into battle in her chariot, wielding a large bow and firing a hail of arrows against a male opponent.[601] There is also evidence that she reigned long enough to send expeditions into Sinai and Palestine as well as initiating building projects, including a large mortuary temple and a royal tomb for herself in the Valley of the Kings.[602]

The ostracon scene, in which a royal figure fires the bow and arrow from a moving chariot in battle, merits a deeper examination. It was found near tomb KV.9 in the Valley of the Kings; dated to the end of the Nineteenth Dynasty (the end of the Ramesside Period), it is a sketch in red and black ink on limestone.[603] Yet the scene could be considered to be unusual, not because of the seeming simplicity of the art, but because the monarch sketched is female, shown riding into battle in her chariot and wielding a large bow with which she fires a hail of arrows against a male opponent.[604] This image has been described as depicting a legend or myth, simply because of the so-called crudity of the drawing.[605] I would disagree both with the concept that the sketch shows a legend and with the argument that the drawing is crude; it is certainly a little simpler than the grand reliefs of some pharaohs, but it is absolutely beautiful in its own way. It has also been suggested that because the horses appear to have about eight legs each, this must be some sort of parody of the traditional depiction of a triumphant pharaoh driving his chariot in battle.[606] Yet this is simply not the case, since this same multiplication of horses' legs is employed in the formal Nineteenth Dynasty temple scenes of both Seti I and his son Ramses II. It seems that this was either the artist's way of depicting the movement of the horse (i.e. the horse galloping) or a second horse behind the first and thereby taking into account the unusual perspective in Egyptian art.

In a war scene of Seti I at Karnak, found on the exterior north wall of the Hypostyle Court, Seti is riding his chariot into battle against the Libyans.[607] At first glance, it appears that there is one horse which has eight legs, yet on closer inspection it is just about possible to make out the second horse's head behind the horse in front. As the Seti war scene is a relief carved into stone, it is easier to see this relatively clearly, likewise the scenes of Ramses II in the interior of his temple at Abu Simbel which again show horses with multiple legs in carved relief. An ink sketch on limestone, such as the aforementioned one of the woman in the chariot, might not be as clear as it is far more likely to have faded over time than a carved relief. It is just as likely that this sketch illustrates an historical figure as it does a mythological figure, an idea that sometimes seems to be more than a little bit difficult for some scholars to grasp.

When examining the date of this sketch, and looking at the history of this particular period in Egypt, it is likely that this drawing does in fact portray the female pharaoh Tawosret.[608] She also appears to have entered into some form of political, if not military, conflict with her male successor Sethnakht, who also usurped her tomb. The image clearly shows a royal woman taking part in active warfare rather than simply playing a symbolic role in the proceedings, as has been suggested by some academics. Although it may well be that this is simply a depiction of a goddess, it still suggests that the Egyptians did at times have some appreciation of the female capacity for combat and violence, and a certain amount of appreciation for women who could multitask so impressively (it's not all that easy to single-handedly drive a chariot and take down some enemies with a bow and arrow). If indeed it does depict the female pharaoh Tawosret, as I certainly believe, it would carry tremendous importance within the bounds of the subject of women and warfare in ancient Egypt.

Women and Warfare

I would argue that the evidence presented here (just a small sample of what there is available so far and what could yet be unearthed in the future) is particularly illuminating in relation to the study of women being involved in warfare and the handling of weaponry to at least some extent. What is apparent is that there are a number of examples of women holding power in ancient Egypt and also assuming military behaviour and styling in certain circumstances, prime examples being the women depicted at Deshasheh and Queen Ahhotep being described as leading her husband's troops into battle. There were also occasions when some women, such as pharaohs Hatshepsut and Nefertiti, are portrayed using weaponry in order to display to their courtiers and subjects their status and their ultimate role as pharaoh.

The examples of Egyptian women wielding military/political power discussed in this book are predominantly female pharaohs and queens, whose roles were obviously significant. However, it is also important to recognise that even non-royal or non-noble ancient Egyptian women had roles of power within society. For example, they had legal and economic independence; they had control of certain economic and religious institutions (such as responsibility for all linen manufacturing) and could also hold administrative positions, with several instances of women throughout Dynastic Egypt holding powerful political offices.[609] If there was such equality in non-royal society, why should it be a surprise that some women held the highest office of the land, such as regent or pharaoh? Or that some women could be involved to some extent in warfare?

The term 'women warriors' is perhaps an overly simplistic one, but one that gets the basic idea across. The combined evidence would certainly suggest that there were some occurrences of women bearing weapons during Egyptian history, with roles ranging from the functional to the ritual or indeed a combination thereof. For example, the image of Nefertiti executing a prisoner can be viewed either as an image of an actual historical event or simply as a way to represent the power she held as co-ruler alongside Akhenaten. Either way, this image, which once adorned temple walls at Amarna, demonstrates the formal acceptance of a woman wielding power over life and death, whether in principle or in fact. In terms of archaeological evidence, mace-heads buried in Predynastic female graves could certainly be argued to be functional objects which the women utilised in life.

By examining ancient Egyptian women, whether royal or not, a series of interesting points have been raised and it is clear that many women throughout ancient Egyptian society have not been as thoroughly studied as they perhaps should have been. There also remains a frustrating dearth of information available for the regrettably lesser-known female pharaohs, such as Neithotep, Sobekneferu, and Tawosret. This appears to be mainly due to the lack of a gender- or feminist-based approach to the subject; the essentialist approach towards gender taken by some archaeologists has long been a problem in archaeology and in Egyptian archaeology in particular.[610] All too often it has been assumed that women in ancient cultures could not take on the roles that are, by modern Western standards, traditionally the domain of men. Women are all too often reduced to being a visual presence, with little consideration by many academics and scholars of the social construction of the body, gender and sexuality.[611] Western cultural constructions do not reflect those of ancient Egypt; by using a gender and feminist approach, the warfare/combat orientated roles that certain women played in different periods of ancient Egyptian culture can be brought to the notice of more people.[612] Examining ancient Egyptian warfare in relation to women has certainly proved frustrating at times, due to the previous lack of studies on the subject and the lack of a sensible gendered approach. It is absolutely necessary for a feminist approach to be taken in order for a reasonably accurate analysis and interpretation of the evidence available in the archaeological and historical record.[613]

There are problems with the past being romanticised, which not only can affect how the public see ancient Egypt but can influence how academics examine the historical record as well. Egyptian Archaeology is one of the sub-disciplines that has been particularly slow to incorporate gender perspectives (particularly in relation to warfare and weaponry) and has suffered from a significant lack of study into the roles available to women. Until relatively recently the majority of work has focused largely on a male elite of kings, priests, and scribes, i.e. the literate 1% of ancient Egyptian society.[614] Work by feminist scholars such as Meskell, Callendar, Troy, and Lesko do address some of these issues within Egyptian archaeology, critiquing past work that has neglected the roles played by women and applying their own analyses to the archaeological evidence available. However, more work still needs to be done. Aspects of Egyptian archaeology do seem to lag behind Archaeology as an overall discipline and this is certainly the case when it comes to taking a gender- or feminist-based approach to the subject.

While the research carried out for this book reveals no evidence whatsoever that ancient Egyptian women were active members of the army at any time in Dynastic history, it is equally clear that women did bear weaponry. This could be as a means to defend themselves (as at Sati), when taking part in ceremonial activities (in the case of female pharaohs), or as a means of demonstrating their status within society (like the weapons found in the burial of Senebtisi). What has hopefully become clear is that much more investigation into the role of women is needed in order to uncover all the information that could be out there.

5

Experimental Archaeology

One way to examine the effectiveness of specific ancient Egyptian weaponry (including possible methods of use, along with potential damage and trauma to those the weapons would have been used against) is to carry out experimental archaeology. Experimental archaeology is an exciting and interesting way of examining the past through the use of artefacts and/or replicas of artefacts. This chapter will first look at the two sets of experiments run by me, before examining the experiments carried out in 2011 by Stonborough.

So why do experimental archaeology?

This set of archaeological experiments were done to assess the effectiveness and functionality of the weapons discussed in this book. The experiments look at a selection of Eighteenth Dynasty weapons; specifically the axe, the dagger, the mace, and the *khopesh*. These experiments were designed to prove definitively that these weapons were functional weapons of combat and to display just how effective such weapons could be.

My experiments were designed to answer the following questions:

- How effective were the axe, the dagger, and the mace as battle weapons?
- What impact would the weapons have? And what damage would they cause to flesh and bone?
- How effective were these weapons when wielded by both men and women?
- Did the damage caused by the weapons wielded by women differ from the damage caused by weapons when wielded by men? If so, what differences were there?

If what has been suggested in the past was true then we would expect to find that none of the weapons, when wielded by untrained people, could cause any significant or disabling damage in combat. As we believed this not to be the case we would count the experiment as successfully proving our ideas if clear and obvious damage could be seen and it would have failed if no discernible damage, beyond superficial cuts and bruising, was done by any of the weapons.

In order to explore these questions replica Egyptian weapons were made for us by skilled craftsmen and then tested on suitable human proxies, pigs. However there are some issues of extrapolation from one species to another and it has been suggested that the proxy used should be approximately the same size as the body it is meant to represent.[615]

Experiment Background.

This experimental archaeology is a continuation and expansion of experiments I carried out during my MA thesis. The work looked at the how effective the mace was as a weapon, particularly when wielded by a woman.[616] The mace-heads that were used were replicas of two of the mace-heads held in the Harrogate Museum (two different mace-head styles: one conical and one piriform) **(Figure 5.1)**. These were created for Professor Joann Fletcher by professional stonemason Matthias Garn of York in 2007.[617] As discussed, one aspect of the MA thesis was examining the use of maces by women, so it was appropriate for the effectiveness to be tested by an adult female (namely, me).[618]

The experiments were carried out using pig heads as human proxies.[619] The head was chosen as the area of the body to test because the experiments were attempting to replicate the smiting scene from Dynastic Egyptian history, in which the blow of the mace was aimed at the victim's head.[620] One important problem noted is that the experiment had to take into account the differences between pig skulls and human skulls. As I found out "a pig skull is approximately two to three times thicker than that of a human, so any damage sustained by a human skull with a blow from a mace would be greater than the damage incurred by the pig skull".[621]

Figure 5.1

The experiments carried out were relatively simple with approximations and estimations being used in order to produce a relevant environment for the tests. For example, I used a metal stand to raise the pig head up to approximately the height of a prisoner kneeling for execution[622] **(Figure 5.2)**. Obviously, as people differ in height, we had to estimate an average height for the pig head to be placed at. Before the experiment was carried out a test pig was used to decide on the best way for wielding the maces (with two hands!) even though this is different from the style portrayed in a typical smiting scene (one handed). Once the initial test was

Figure 5.2

completed, and a blow style selected, the individual maces were then assessed and the entire experiment documented through photography and video.[623]

The results produced by this set of experiments were extremely interesting. Prior to the experiment, I believed that the globular mace-head would be the most

Figure 5.3

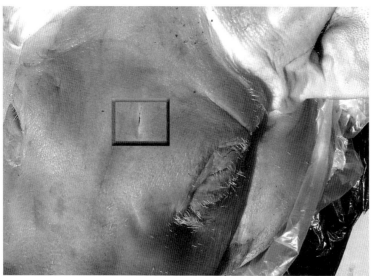

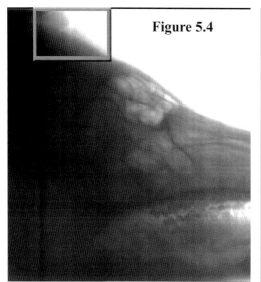

Figure 5.4

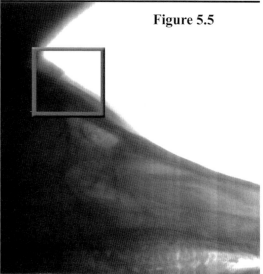

Figure 5.5

effective, expecting the blunt force trauma of such a weapon to break the bones of the skull with relative ease. It is also the one that is most commonly depicted in the ancient Egyptian smiting scenes, so this seemed to suggest that this was the style of mace that was preferred by the ancient Egyptians.

Yet, this turned out not to be the case. The conical mace-head actually split the skin of the pig head, whilst the globular mace caused no visible damage to the skin[624] **(Figure 5.3)**. Subsequent X-rays of the two main test skulls revealed the impact of each mace even more clearly. The X-ray of the pig head hit with the globular mace showed some slight cracking and damage to the skull of the pig, though not as much as was perhaps expected[625] **(Figure 5.4)**. The X-ray of the pig head hit by the conical

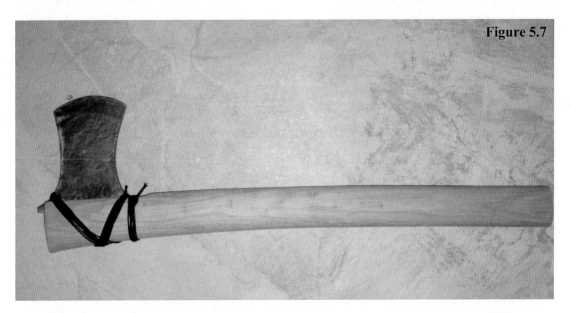

Figure 5.7

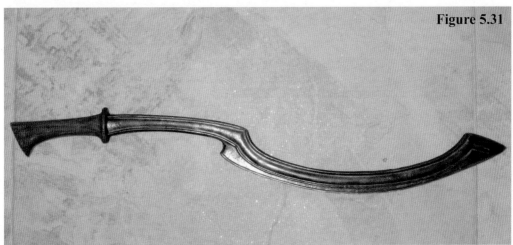

Figure 5.31

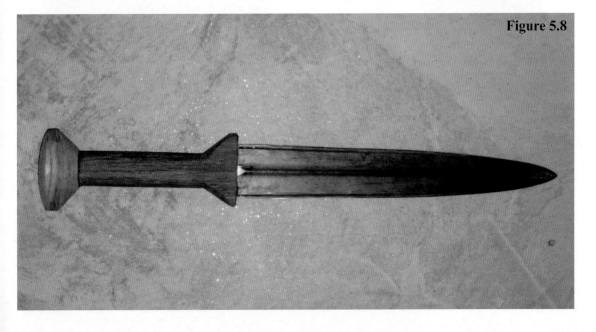

Figure 5.8

Figure 5.10

Figure 5.11

Figure 5.12

Figure 5.32

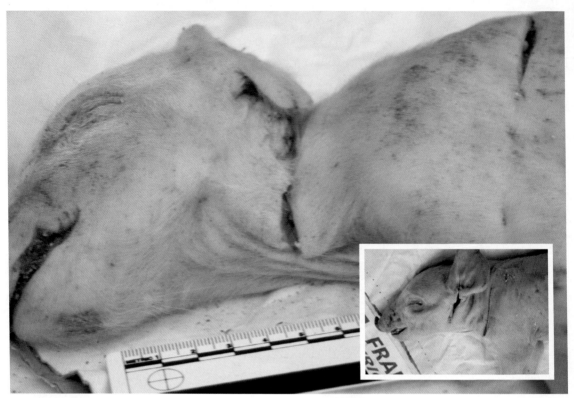

Figure 5.33 (inset), Figure 5.34 (top)

Figure 5.35

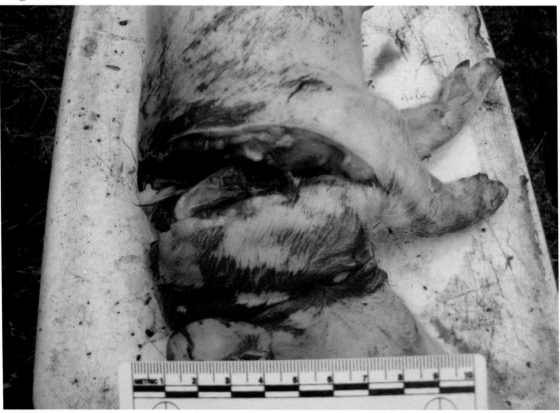

Figure 5.36

Figure 5.38

Figure 5.37

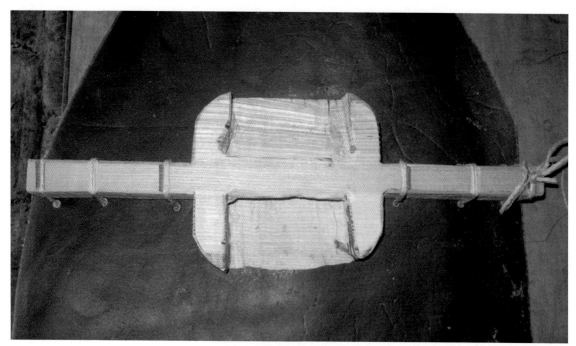

Figure 5.38

Figure 5.39

Figure 5.40

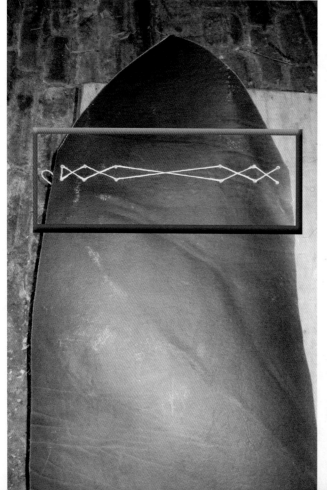

Figure 5.41

Figure 5.42

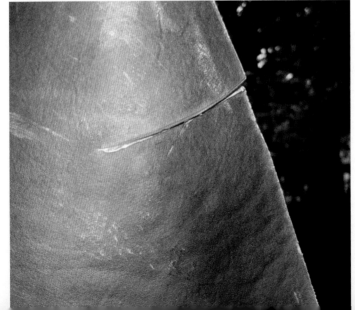

Figure 5.44

Figure 5.43

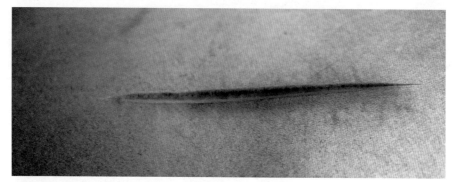

Figure 5.45

Figure 5.46

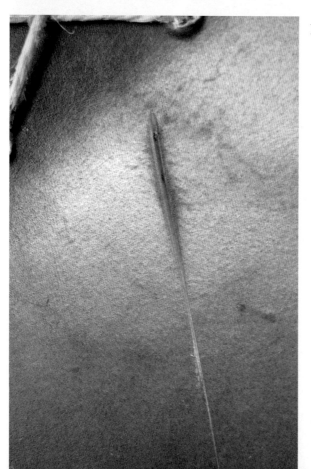

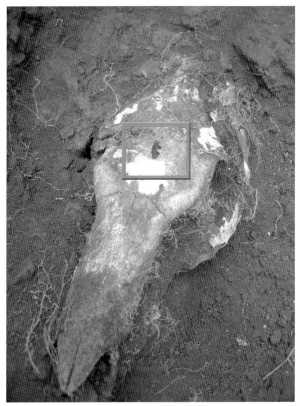

Figure 5.6

mace, however, showed damage that was more extensive than the damage caused by the globular mace and there is evidence of damage to the skull, where there is a sizeable crack (almost a 'step') in the bone[626] **(Figure 5.5)**. These results suggest the possibility that the globular mace was portrayed more often in smiting scenes due to it simply representing the 'mace' in a generic sense, rather than it being an exact depiction.

After the experiments and X-rays had been carried out in 2009, the pig heads were buried in soil, at a depth of approximately four feet, at the archaeological excavation site of Heslington East in North Yorkshire. Unfortunately I was only able to retrieve one of the pig skulls later on (I believe the other had been dug up and carried-off by a fox at some stage!). The pig skull struck with the conical mace-head was the skull I exhumed two years later in July of 2011, when the skull had become completely de-fleshed and therefore the damage caused by the conical mace clearly visible **(Figure 5.6)**. The sizeable hole created by the mace-head was impressive and provided yet further evidence for its effectiveness.[627]

What this showed me was that the conical mace-head was the more effective of the two weapon shapes, causing the most amount of damage (seen on both the X-Ray and the de-fleshed skull) on the individual mace-head tests. The globular mace-head would also have caused substantial damage to a human skull if wielded with sufficient force; however, the sharp edge of the conical mace-head gave it the advantage when it came to damaging both the skin and the skull.[628]

One thing which really stood out was the amount of damage that a relatively small weapon could cause, even though pigs skulls were used.[629] The thinner skulls of sheep would have been closer in thickness to human skulls, though these are not available to the public in the same way that pig skulls are.[630] It is likely that worse damage would be achieved if the maces came in contact with sheep or human skulls but the results from the pig skulls show just how dangerous they could be even when wielded by a woman completely untrained in the art of warfare.[631]

Weaponry Choice

The weapons chosen for this round of experimental archaeology were a mace, a dagger, an axe, and a *khopesh*. The *khopesh* was used in a slightly different experiment (discussed later) to the axe, dagger, and mace. The mace used was the same as the conical mace used in 2009. These are all weapons which can be associated with ancient Egyptian women, either as burial goods or in visual portrayals. Three of the weapons used in the experimental archaeology (the axe, the dagger, and the *khopesh*) were cast by Neil Burridge, who is an experienced bronze swordsmith based in Cornwall. Specialising in ancient bronze swords and other ancient bronze weapons, he has worked with archaeologists in the past[632] and was extremely interested in this particular project, taking a considerable amount of time to cast the three Eighteenth Dynasty replica weapons required for this experimental archaeology.

The Axe

The axe-head commissioned for this is a replica of an axe-head featured in Davies' *Catalogue of Ancient Antiquities in the British Museum. VIII. Tools and Weapons I. Axes* (1987). This was axe 123, number EA.67589, an Eighteenth Dynasty axe-head found at Amarna.[633] The bronze alloy for the axe contained 9% tin to the copper, which according to Neil Burridge is generally consistent with the bronze weapon alloys of the period. Davies' metallurgic analysis of the original axe-head (123) revealed that it contained 90.6% copper, and 7.9% tin, with trace amounts of other metals.[634] Therefore, it was decided that the 9% tin content of the axe-head made by Neil Burridge was an appropriate amount.

The replica axe-head was then hafted by Neil Raval of Macclesfield, using a hickory axe-handle. Whilst axe hafts in ancient Egypt would not be made of hickory wood (which is predominantly found in North America, India, and China), it was felt that hickory was an appropriate substitute for native Egyptian woods such as acacia, which is not easily obtainable in Britain. The haft was cut to length of 44.1 cm, a length based on another Eighteenth Dynasty axe handle from Davies' catalogue, axe 117.[635] The haft was then finished with Danish oil and the head attached to the haft by slotting it into a groove cut into the wood. This was then secured with leather ties and the axe head itself was later treated with ballistol oil, helping to prevent corrosion **(Figure 5.7 – see plates).**

The Dagger

The dagger commissioned is a replica of an Eighteenth Dynasty (c.1560BC) dagger of Ahmose I, the founder of the Eighteenth Dynasty. This dagger, held in the Royal Ontario Museum in Toronto, Canada, was found at Abydos by Charles Currelly, the founder of this museum. The dagger was composed of bronze, with a limestone pommel. At the top of the pommel was a cartouche bearing the name of Ahmose I in gold.[636]

Neil Burridge had made this replica previously, so was therefore experienced in casting another such weapon **(Figure 5.8 – see plates)**. The bronze alloy again contained 9% tin, consistent with the bronze weapon alloys of the period. This was completed with the wooden hilt and a pommel likewise made of wood rather than limestone. The gold nails and detailing were felt unnecessary for a replica to be used for experimental archaeology, so the hilt was simply sanded down and treated with ballistol oil.

Methodology

Stonborough's (2011) experiments (discussed below) demonstrated the effectiveness, or arguably the lack thereof, of the *khopesh* and axe against a rawhide shield. I, on the other hand, went for a very different test subject for the weaponry: pig carcasses

Figure 5.9

as human proxies. After consultation with Professor Joann Fletcher, Dr Stephen Buckley, and Professor Terry O'Connor (all of the University of York), it was decided that sections of belly pork with the ribs still attached would be the best option for testing. These sections of belly pork retained the pig skin, fat, and muscle on top of the ribs **(Figure 5.9)** with the layer of skin, fat, and muscle approximately one to two inches in depth, varying slightly for each section. This was felt to reflect human chest anatomy sufficiently to show whether the weapons had the capacity to fracture ribs or to penetrate to underlying organs.

Three individuals were selected to carry out a test of each weapon, producing twelve results in total. For the initial tests of the axe, dagger, and mace, nine sections of belly pork (three ribs wide) were procured from the butcher G. A. Swains of York and the experiments took place in the garden of a private residence. A consultation with Thom Richardson, **Keeper of Armour and Oriental Collections at the Royal Armouries Museum** in Leeds, helped assess how the weapons could best be wielded in the experiments. The sections of pig were placed on a sheet of plastazote to provide support and this in turn placed on the flat top of a raised plastic stand to a height of approximately one metre. Each pig section was struck with three blows from each weapon. The participants are named P1 (Participant One, female), P2 (Participant Two, male), and P3 (Participant 3, female). The first letter of the weapon name is added on for each experiment, for example my test of the axe is named 'P1A'.

The axe strikes carried out by each participant were all two-handed and targeted at the pig sections both parallel with the ribs and across the ribs. Each participant struck the ribs three times. A two-handed strike was employed rather than a one-handed strike, as this was felt to be a style of blow that was easier to control and produced more power than a one-handed blow **(Figure 5.10 – see plates)**.

The mace blows were targeted at the pig sections parallel to the ribs and across the ribs. Each person struck the pig section three times with the mace, again using a two-handed strike **(Figure 5.11 – see plates)**.

The dagger experiments were slightly different from the axe and mace experiments. Although each participant again produced three strikes at the pig sections, the aim of the dagger testing was to examine its effectiveness as a close-quarters weapon. Therefore, two of the tests simply slid the dagger gently between the ribs three times. The final test, however, also included a more forceful strike, diagonally across the ribs, in order to compare what damage would result if the dagger were used with more force **(Figure 5.12 – see plates)**.

Following two days' refrigeration, the pig sections were X-rayed at the Archaeology Department of the University of York, at the King's Manor. The X-ray equipment was a Hewlett Packard Faxitron Cabinet X-ray System, the settings used were 60kv 1mA(3) 40ms, and the digital images produced by an NTB Digital X-ray scanner EZ40.

Observations and Results

The Axe

The P1A test produced immediately observable results **(Figure 5.13)**. On two of the strikes that hit across the ribs, the axe sliced through the layers of skin, fat, and muscle with relative ease when striking towards the edge of the pig section closest

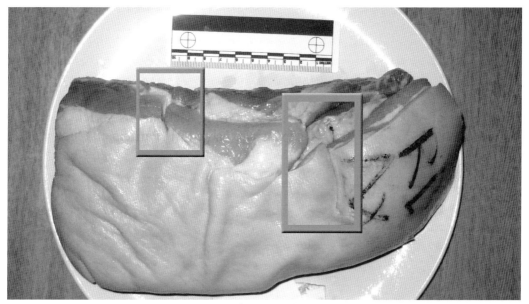

Figure 5.13

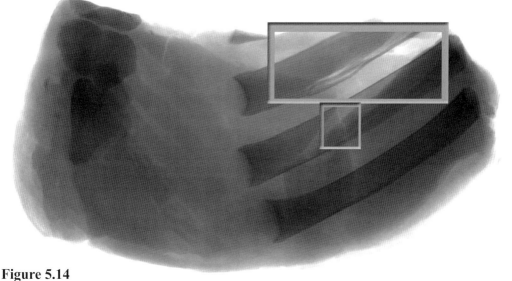

Figure 5.14

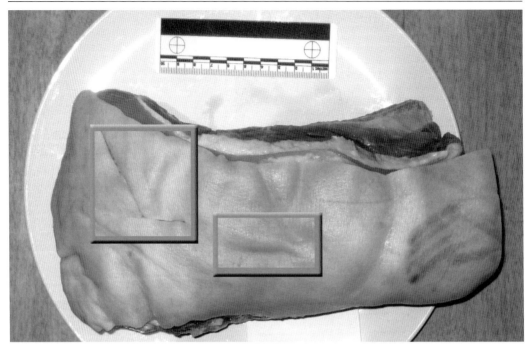

Figure 5.15

to the tester. The third strike, hitting parallel to the ribs, did not actually break the skin or pierce the pig flesh in any way. The X-ray of ribs with the P1A strikes produced some very interesting results **(Figure 5.14)**; not only was some soft tissue damage visible on the X-ray, but the middle rib had a distinct transverse fracture[637] running across the width of the rib. Another rib bone, at the bottom of the X-ray

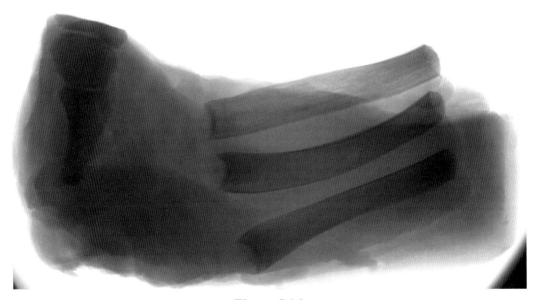

Figure 5.16

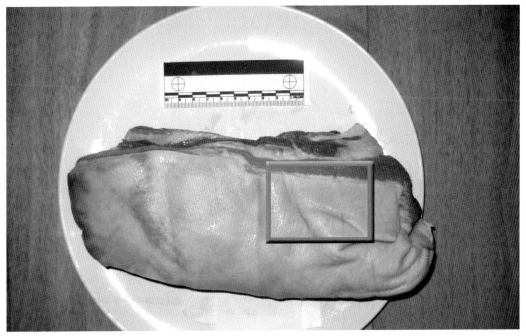

Figure 5.17

(closest to where the tester had been standing when delivering the blows) had a section that had shattered vertically along the edge of the bone, in what appears to be a comminuted fracture.[638]

The P2A test **(Figure 5.15)** had two strikes that cut into the skin and flesh: one strike parallel to the ribs and the other diagonally across the ribs. A third strike did not break or pierce the soft tissue in any way. The X-ray of the ribs with P2A'S strikes produced some perhaps unexpected results, particularly when considering the X-ray of P1A – there was no visible damage to the rib bones at all **(Figure 5.16)**.

The P3A test, contrary to the two other axe tests, showed nothing initially **(Figure 5.17)**. None of the strikes, either parallel or across the ribs, either broke the skin or

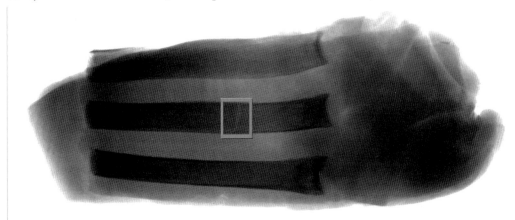

Figure 5.18

pierced the flesh, leaving only indentations where the axe-head had hit. However, the X-ray of the P3A tests produced an interesting result; the middle rib bone alone clearly displayed a distinct transverse fracture[639] horizontally across the rib bone **(Figure 5.18).**

The Mace

The P1M test, contrary to two of the axe tests, produced no immediately observable results **(Figure 5.19)**. None of the three strikes, parallel to the ribs or hitting across the ribs, broke the skin or pierced the flesh, though there were a couple

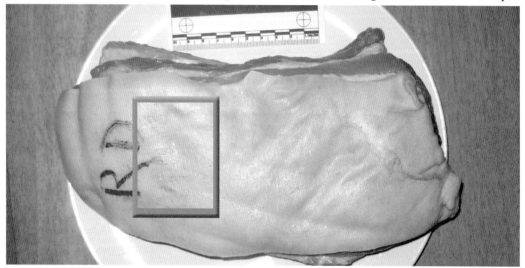

Figure 5.19

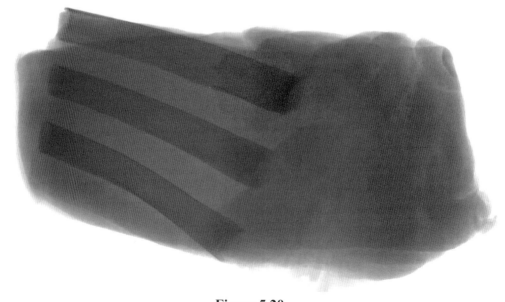

Figure 5.20

of indentations on the skin from where the mace hit. The X-ray of the P1M tests showed no sign of damage to any of the rib bones whatsoever **(Figure 5.20)**. While this result may have been, at first, disappointing, it did provide evidence as to the effect of the mace when struck against a body part with much thicker soft tissue (muscle and fat) than the skull.

The P2M test results were similar to P1M. Again, none of the three strikes, whether parallel to the ribs or hitting across the ribs, broke the skin or pierced the flesh, although, as with P1M, there were a couple of indentations on the skin where the mace hit (**Figure 5.21**). The X-ray of the P2M tests, as with P1M, showed no sign of damage to any of the rib bones whatsoever (**Figure 5.22**).

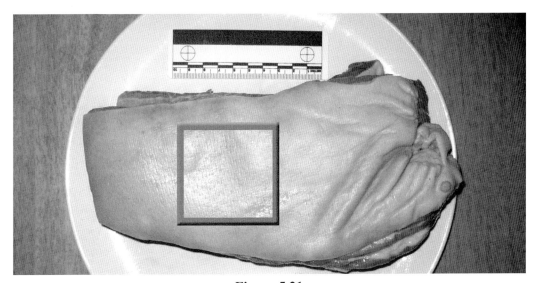

Figure 5.21

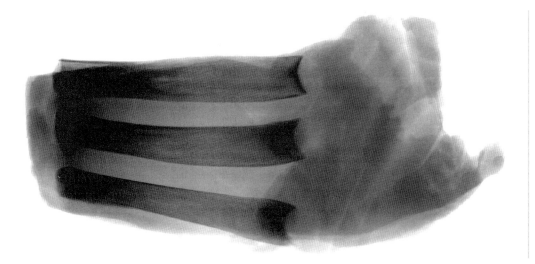

Figure 5.22

The P3M test result again was similar to P1M and P2M. Once again, none of the three strikes, whether parallel to the ribs or hitting across the ribs, broke the skin or pierced the flesh, although, as with tests P1M and P2M, there were a couple of indentations on the skin from the impact **(Figure 5.23)**. None of the ribs in the X-ray of the P3M tests, as with P1M and P2M tests, showed any visible signs of damage **(Figure 5.24)**.

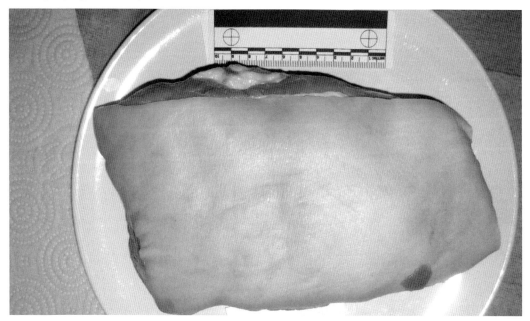

Figure 5.23

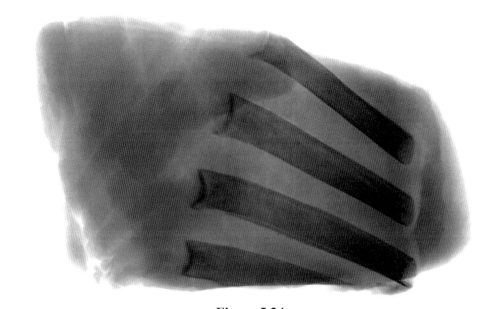

Figure 5.24

The Dagger

The P1D test had immediately observable results **(Figure 5.25)**. The three 'hits' with the dagger, parallel to the rib bones, were extremely effective: the dagger blade cut through six centimetres of pig skin, fat, and muscle, going straight through between the ribs with no discernible resistance. The underside of the pig section even displayed damage, demonstrating that the dagger would have penetrated the body cavity, damaging underlying organs. Although the X-ray of P1D showed no

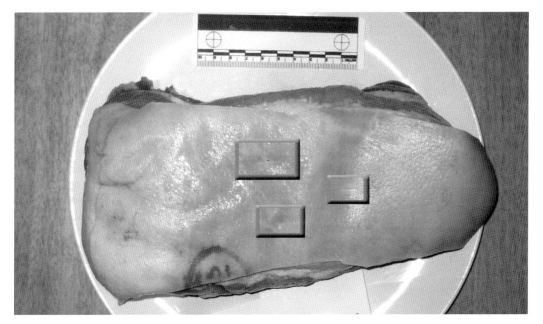

Figure 5.25

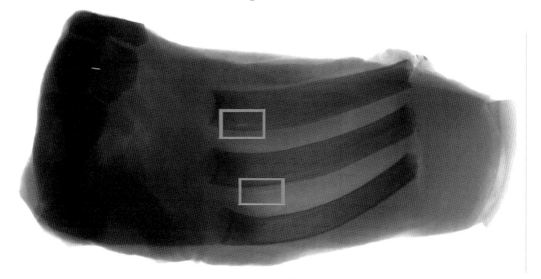

Figure 5.26

sign of significant damage to any of the rib bones, the tip of the dagger blade had scratched the top of one rib **(Figure 5.26)**. The X-ray also clearly showed the wound tract for at least one of the dagger blows.

The P2D, as with P1D, also had instant results **(Figure 5.27)**. The two 'hits' with the dagger, both parallel to the rib bones, had again been extremely effective. As with test P1D, the dagger blade cut through over six centimetres of skin, fat, and muscle, and straight through between the ribs with no discernible resistance. The X-ray of the P2D tests showed no evidence of damage to any of the rib bones but

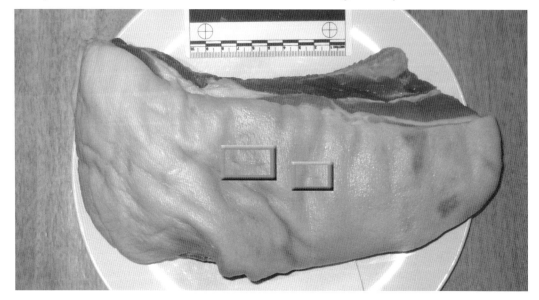

Figure 5.27

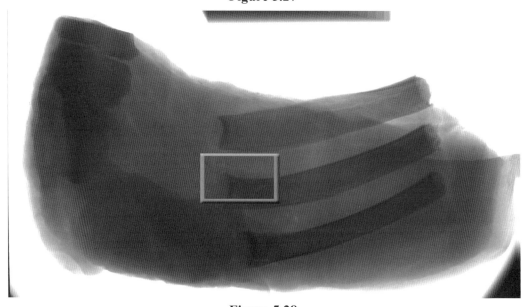

Figure 5.28

did show the wound tract for at least one of the dagger blows **(Figure 5.28)**, which again displays just how brutally effective this particular style of dagger could be.

The P3D test, as with tests P1D and P2D, also had an immediate visual effect **(Figure 5.29)**. The first two relatively gentle 'hits' with the dagger, one of which was parallel to the ribs whilst the other was diagonal, were again extremely effective. As with the two other dagger tests, the blade cut easily straight through between the ribs with no discernible resistance. The third dagger blow was done with much more force and from a greater height than the other two tests. The X-ray of P3D showed the wound tracts for the two initial blows, including where the tip of the dagger blade had scratched the top of the rib bone **(Figure 5.30)**. Yet the most interesting result from the X-ray of P3D was the result of the third, more forceful

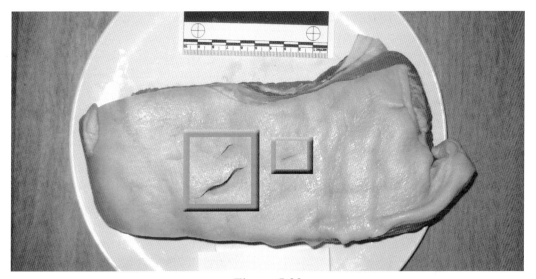

Figure 5.29

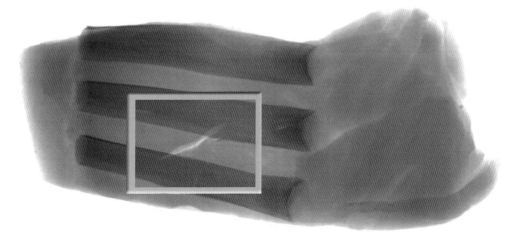

Figure 5.30

blow. Not only was a much larger wound tract clearly visible, but the dagger blow (which had fallen diagonally between two rib bones) had damaged the rib bones on either side of the wound tract, chipping the bone.

Analysis

It is usually the case that the most common indications of trauma and injury in the archaeological record are bone fractures in skeletal remains.[640] While this may indeed be the case for most archaeological examples, in the case of Egyptian remains (which were often intentionally mummified or preserved in the arid environment) the soft tissue is also preserved. This of course allows for any damage to this tissue to be observed and comparisons made between experimental archaeology results and any examples of damage found on the relevant mummified remains (e.g. Seqenenre, the Slain Soldiers of Montu-hotep etc).

When examining the damage caused by the different weapon tests, certain factors have to be taken into account. In terms of bones, blunt force trauma (such as that seen in the mace experiments) can create a wide range of fracture patterns which are determined by the instrument (or specific weapon) used to inflict the damage.[641] Also for these experiments the test subjects were pig rather than human bone and fracture pathways are in part determined by the design and composition of the bone involved, including morphology and density.[642] It is also generally accepted that, especially in forensic anthropology trauma analysis, it is difficult to develop and carry out such studies because of the dearth of suitable samples of study material.[643] Due to a lack of readily available (or willing) human samples for these experiments, the factors involved in using pig remains have to be taken into account.

As is necessary in experiments such as these, it is essential to match the nature of human bone as much as possible in order to ensure the most accurate results; however, using actual live human material would naturally be frowned upon by most observers.[644] As discussed previously, pig flesh and bone were considered the best human proxy of the options available. Of course, Galloway *et al.*[645] are discussing experimental work relation to forensics and presenting forensic tests and results in a court case. However, this is something that must be appreciated when assessing and analysing the results of these experiments.

The Axe

The photographs and X-rays of the pig sections hit by the axe show some varied results. At times, the axe worked as a both cutting and a clubbing impact weapon (see example P1A), cutting the flesh easily and producing a shock load sufficient to break bone with its impact on the ribs. This caused both a transverse fracture on one rib and a comminuted fracture on another. The occurrence of a comminuted fracture is interesting, as this type of fracture is generally caused through the use of great force, perhaps even in the form of a crushing injury.[646] Therefore, the presence of such a fracture in the X-ray of a pig section hit with a blow from an axe suggests that the weapon indeed has crushing capabilities and was perhaps hit with more force by the participant testing the weapon.

P1A is the only test example where both some soft tissue trauma and a bone-break occurred. Example P3A broke a rib bone with a transverse fracture, but did not cut through the flesh of the pig at all. Example P2A was the opposite; there was plenty of soft tissue damage from the cutting axe blade but no damage at all to the rib bones. These diverse results would suggest that the impact and effectiveness of the axe as a weapon is subject to the individual wielding the weapon. It is possible that the results vary according to how closely to a 90 degree angle the axe-edge hits the skin. If the axe is tilted slightly it may cut in obliquely, thereby rapidly dissipating the force of the blow. It is also possible that in the case of test P1A, the soft tissue damage was so extensive due to the axe blade striking at the edge of the pig section rather than in the centre. This could have meant that the axe blade would cut through the soft tissue more easily, with less resistance than if it had struck the centre. In each case, however, it is apparent that the axe is extremely effective as a weapon, whether it is wielded by a man or a woman.

The axe, even when tested by untrained individuals, caused serious soft tissue damage through large slashes in the skin and muscle (which could potentially cause fatal blood loss if the right area was struck) or had enough impact to break bone. Either way, it could cause a debilitating injury to the individual receiving such a blow. On one occasion (P1A) it did both, suggesting that this style of axe would have been a formidable weapon in Eighteenth Dynasty warfare.

The Mace

As the results of the experiments with the mace reveal, there was no evidence of any bone damage in any of the three tests carried out. This is not necessarily an unexpected occurrence: the depth of other tissues, such as the skin, fat, and muscle, would disperse some of the force and impact of the blunt force trauma from the mace.[647] There is such a notable difference between the initial 2009 tests on the pig skull and the 2011 tests on the rib cage sections precisely because of the difference in depth of the soft tissue. In the 2009 experiment, the depth of the soft tissue on the pig skull was sufficiently minimal to allow the conical mace to not only split the skin, but to provide enough force to penetrate the soft tissue and cause substantial damage to the skull itself. The conical mace would appear to combine blunt- and sharp-force trauma in one weapon. This is not to say that the lack of bone damage to the rib section meant that the mace had no effect at all. The impact of such blunt force trauma would have caused a great deal of muscle damage, a potentially incapacitating injury. The layer of muscle and fat overlaying a human ribcage can be less than that of the pig ribcage, so the damage caused to a human by a mace blow could be more extensive than these experiments showed.

Neither the gender of the test participant nor the force with which the mace struck the pig section appears to have any effect on the damage caused, or lack thereof. These initial experiments suggest that the mace may not always have been a particularly useful weapon in a battlefield situation. Both the axe and the mace would be equally effective as a clubbing weapon but the axe would have had the added advantage of the sharp edge. The mace is a weapon that would have more impact when striking a skull, therefore making it an ideal choice for executions. This may be one reason as to why the mace is represented so prolifically in ancient Egyptian smiting scenes.

The Dagger

In the experiments with the dagger, X-ray images of the tests P1D and P2D showed little more than the wound tracts created by the dagger blade and an example of a scrape mark across the surface of one of the ribs in P1D of the type identified by White and Folkens.[648] The experiments revealed that the dagger can easily pierce skin, fat, and muscle and would easily penetrate vital organs with little effort required. Simply sliding the dagger gently between the ribs was enough to cause a large amount of soft tissue damage. The most fascinating result, however, came from test P3D, where the third dagger strike using more force than the first two strikes produced significant bone damage, thereby demonstrating the potential of even the lightest and most delicate of bronze blades.

This damage to the rib bones caused by the dagger reflects the occurrences of bone damage as described by Mays, where bone fractures are sometimes seen at cuts due to a sharp weapon slicing the bone itself; these are usually indicative of an assault.[649] This slicing of the bone is definitely evident in the X-rays of the P3D tests; the way in which the bone was damaged related to the fact that the pig remains were extremely fresh, having been butchered the day before the experiments. This slicing, rather than shattering, of the bone is due to the freshness of the remains ensuring that the bone has retained its organic resilience.[650] So the freshness of the pig remains ensured that the damage caused by the blows of the dagger and the other weapons were relatively similar to the peri-mortem damage sustained by humans in combat situations.

Again, there are differences in rib bone densities between pigs and humans (although they are a good match in size), but it is reasonable to postulate that the dagger would cause very similar damage to a human rib bone, if used with enough force and speed. The ease with which damage was caused to the thicker soft tissue of the pig sections only highlights how the damage to human soft tissue of lesser thickness could be more extensive.

Conclusions

The results of these experiments were most enlightening. The axe and the dagger certainly inflicted significant injury to the pig remains. The results did differ between the participants but it would be difficult to argue that this was due to gender. It seems rather more likely to be due to the differences in the techniques each one employed. Whilst the mace may not have been particularly effective in this set of experiments, it had already been proved to be an effective weapon when it comes into contact with a skull. As discussed above, whilst the mace may not be been the most battle-appropriate weapon, the axe and dagger could potentially have highly useful in combat; the axe as both a clubbing and hacking weapon and the dagger as a last-resort, close-quarters combat weapon. It would also be very difficult to argue that these weapons were purely votive items rather than functional weapons.

Photographs of the axe and dagger trauma display the soft tissue injuries very clearly. The dagger trauma does not appear to differ in relation to the gender or experience of the participant. The extent of the damage suggests it would be easy for the dagger blade to pierce skin and muscle and seriously injure vital organs, making it a dangerous weapon in anyone's hands and very effective in combat. It is evident that little to no training would be required to use such a blade successfully; the skill in using the dagger in a battlefield situation would lie in getting close enough to an enemy to be able to stick it in. The axe had less success in cutting through the soft tissue but was still effective in cutting skin and muscle in two of the experiments. As discussed above, the angle at which the axe blade struck the pig skin appears to have had an effect on the amount of damage done, possibly indicating that using one is a skill that must be learnt. The mace is a different prospect. The photographs of the mace tests show no soft tissue damage other than a few dents in the pig skin. The mace would certainly inflict some damage but not necessarily sufficient damage to completely incapacitate a victim.

The X-rays nonetheless demonstrate the damage which was caused to the bones by the other weapons. The effectiveness of the axe in experiment P1A is reflected in the shattered bone and transverse fractures which clearly demonstrate the clubbing ability of the axe, even when wielded by an untrained person. The same type of transverse fracture can be seen in the X-rays of experiment P3A demonstrating that the axe damage to bone is consistent. As the X-rays of the mace experiments showed no bone damage, little can be assessed other than the fact that the mace was ineffective against bone when a good layer of skin, tissue, and muscle is present.

The X-rays of the dagger experiments, as discussed previously, were very different from the results of both the axe and mace experiments. Most of the tests show little to no bone damage caused by the dagger but the X-ray of experiment P3D shows that the dagger blade could in fact damage bone significantly if wielded with enough force. While the slicing of the bone in this instance may not represent the most incapacitating of injuries, it nonetheless suggests that the dagger does have the potential to do serious damage to bone as well as soft tissue.

The experiments carried out demonstrate that these weapons, which were associated with women in some form, could indeed serve as functional items. The effectiveness of the mace was initially displayed in 2009, but it has now been demonstrated that the damage done can be limited depending on which part of the body it strikes. The axe and the dagger were the two weapons that displayed the most interesting and informative results. Evidently it can be strongly argued that the dagger and axe were not purely for decoration or symbolism but could have been used, effectively, by women as functional weapons. The evidence is less straight-forwards for the mace as it seems to have been far more devastating when used for execution rather than combat.

These experiments were designed to show that ancient Egyptian women were physically able to employ the weapons associated with them throughout ancient Egyptian history, such as the weapons found in various burials and the blades seen in visual representations. As considered previously, gender or biological sex appears not to have been a factor in the damage the weapons caused; there is no reason to think that the supposedly lesser muscularity of women would have rendered them unable to use these weapons to lethal or disabling effect. The scenes depicted at Deshasheh demonstrate that ancient Egyptian women might well utilise weaponry (and to great effect, visually at least) when under threat and the experiments carried out here support this.

The *Khopesh*

Although the experiments testing the replica *khopesh* differed from those employed for the axe, mace, and dagger in order to reflect the way in which the *khopesh* was used, the research questions for the *khopesh* were similar to those posed for the other weapons, i.e.:

- Could the *khopesh* have inflicted significant injury, thereby demonstrating its use as a genuine combat weapon rather than a symbolic or token object?
- How effective would the *khopesh* be in battle?
- What is the impact of the *khopesh* on both the soft tissue and bone of the neck and spinal column?
- How effective was the *khopesh* when wielded by both sexes, on the basis that the amount of force employed by each would differ?

- How variable was the damage inflicted by the *khopesh* when wielded by women as opposed to men? If so, what differences were there?

The Weapon

The *khopesh* selected for replication was the 'Greater *Khopesh*' found among the burial goods of Tutankhamun **(Figure 5.31 – see plates)**. Although Carter found two of these swords in Tutankhamun's tomb, only one was suitable for the experimental research, namely the larger, heavier example found amongst single sticks.[651] As described earlier, both swords had the blade, the shaft, and the handle cast in one single piece. Carter describes the larger of these two weapons as having been designed for crushing rather than cutting and this larger *khopesh* could have inflicted significant wounds due to the sheer weight of the blade.[652]

Experienced in producing such weapons, metalworker and weapons expert Neil Burridge has been casting replicas of this larger *khopesh* for several years.[653] The *khopesh* commissioned for this research was cast from a bronze alloy containing 12% tin, thereby replicating the type of metal employed in New Kingdom weaponry. The weapon was also supplied with a wooden hilt, subsequently sanded down and treated with shellac in order to protect the wood and make it easier to handle; a treatment not inconsistent with New Kingdom practices although different substances may have been used. Both the blade and the hilt have also been treated with ballistol oil, as in the case with the weaponry used in the previous experiments.

Methodology

After consultation with Thom Richardson of the Royal Armouries Leeds, it was decided to design a slightly different experiment for testing the *khopesh*. The experiment is based on the well-known Eighteenth Dynasty representation of a woman using a *khopesh*, i.e. the smiting scene involving Nefertiti and a prisoner. As with other swords throughout history, I believe that the *khopesh* would have been used to sever vital arteries or even decapitate the prisoner rather than simply wildly strike them about the head. Therefore using the same style of experiment as employed for the axe, dagger, and mace was not appropriate for the testing of the *khopesh*. The most suitable proxies for this experiment were piglet carcasses of approximately 35-40cm in length, in this case supplied by Shedden Farm, York. The same three participants from the previous experiments were chosen to carry out the tests with the *khopesh*.

The experiments took place in the grounds of a private residence. As discussed above, Thom Richardson of the Royal Armouries helped me to decide how the *khopesh* could best be wielded in the experiments. However, on the first day of the experiment the farm were only able to provide two of the three piglets requested.

Therefore it was decided that only the two female participants (P1K & P3K) should carry out the experiments at this time and the third and final *khopesh* test, carried out by a male participant (P2K), was slightly postponed until further carcasses became available.

As with the previous experiments, the *khopesh* experiment took place outdoors with plenty of natural light and each stage of the experiment photographed. The piglets were raised on a plastic stand to a height of approximately one metre, thereby replicating the approximate height of the neck of a kneeling human adult. Each piglet was then struck with three blows from the *khopesh*. The strikes carried out by each participant were a combination of one-handed and two-handed strokes, and struck the piglets on the area of the neck and the shoulder as seen in the images.

Results

In experiment P1K, the piglet corpse was struck three times with the *khopesh*, twice with a one-handed strike and once with a two-handed strike **(Figure 5.32 – see plates)**. The first blow to the shoulder area easily cut through skin, fat, and muscle and produced a large, clean, straight-edged wound. The second blow hit the neck area at the jawline and caused significant damage to the neck while also cutting into the piglet's ear. The third blow (the two-handed blow) caught the shoulder and the top of the front leg **(Figure 5.33 – see plates)**.

In experiment P3K, the piglet corpse was again struck three times with the *khopesh* (twice with a one-handed strike and once with a two-handed strike). The first blow was to the shoulder area and, as with experiment P1K, easily cut through skin, fat, and muscle where the top section of the blade had struck. There was also a smaller cut a little further down the area where the blade had hit. The second blow hit the neck area behind the ear and caused some damage to the neck, cutting away the skin to an extent of approximately 2 square centimetres. The third blow (two-handed) hit the neck area again and caused significant damage, cutting deeply into the neck **(Figure 5.34 – see plates)**.

To keep things consistent, in experiment P2K, the piglet corpse was struck three times with the *khopesh*, twice with a one-handed strike and once with a two-handed strike. The first blow was to the neck area and, as with the first two experiments, it cut through skin, fat, and muscle (which produced a significant amount of blood!) in the area where the middle section of the blade had struck. The second blow hit the shoulder area and caused extensive damage, cutting into the body by several centimetres. The third blow (two-handed) hit the shoulder area again and caused significant damage, cutting deeply into the shoulder area and almost all the way through the animal's body **(Figure 5.35 – see plates)**.

Analysis and Conclusions

As highlighted in the photographs, the *khopesh* sword is capable of inflicting a great deal of trauma to soft tissue, even when wielded by inexperienced participants. Only a very small exertion of force was required to produce the trauma results observed. Even without the use of X-Rays, it was obvious that the damage caused at the neck area would have proved fatal, due to the severing of key arteries leading to serious blood loss. Piglets were used as a proxy because they have a similar neck diameter and thickness of skin to a human. It is therefore possible to extrapolate that the damage sustained by a human neck on the receiving end of such a strike would have been very similar, if not the same. Although complete decapitation did not result, the depth of the cuts to the neck would have severed the common carotid or external carotid artery, and cuts to the shoulder are likely to have cut the subclavian artery. An adult human victim would be unconscious within one minute and dead from loss of blood within about three minutes.[654]

The trauma sustained by the piglets was most severe at the neck area, suggesting that aiming a strike at a human neck would be the most efficient and effective way to employ the *khopesh*. As a weapon, the *khopesh*, with its remarkably sharp-edged and curved blade, seems designed for slashing rather than clubbing. It was also quite tricky to handle, even cumbersome at times, due to the curved nature and the weight of the blade. The way in which the sword was not well-balanced for complete ease of handling suggests it would not have been a particularly practical weapon for large-scale battle encounters. Therefore, it could be said that the *khopesh* was not a weapon fashioned for the battlefield (unlike later curved blades such as the scimitar, which were better balanced), but rather more for close-combat situations e.g. 'one-on-one' combat prowess displays or formal executions, as characterised in the aforementioned Nefertiti smiting scene. The graceful form and shape of the *khopesh* would also appear impressive when used in such executions, adding a somewhat aesthetic, as well as injurious, characteristic to the weapon.

As discussed earlier, the gender of the user does not seem to affect the damage that the weapons can cause. These experiments showed conclusively that the *khopesh* can have a lethal impact even in the hands of untrained individuals regardless of biological sex or gender. The cultural conditioning that has been seen in the work of many Western archaeologists (who have long ignored the importance of taking women in the past seriously) is something that this book sets out to challenge and the experimental archaeology carried out here is one important element of that. Many academics in past (and at times not too distant past!) made the assumption that women could not have possibly used such weapons effectively because that was not the sort of role that should be allocated to their assigned 'gender'; regardless of the fact that ancient Egyptian culture would not have the same social roles and customs that a modern Western culture has. As stated above, these experiments set out to prove (and I would argue here that it has been proven successfully) that ancient Egyptian women had the physical abilities to use certain weapons effectively and with relative ease, even with a lack of training. It should not have been necessary to have to carry out such experiments, but a point had to be made in order to counteract the outmoded assumptions made by certain academics with regard to women within the archaeological and historical record.

Shields

The following section is reproduced, with permission, from William Stonborough's 2011 work. Stonborough carried out a set of experiments similar to those carried out by this author, only they surrounded the design and use of a replica shield in relation to the weapon types used here.

As Stonborough has pointed out, there are inconsistencies in the current understanding of the materials, construction, and effectiveness of a lot of the defensive military equipment, particularly shields, from Dynastic Egypt.[655] It is likely that shields were probably the most widely used item of protective equipment in ancient Egyptian warfare, due to the frequency of their portrayals in battle scenes.[656] This lack of consistency, along with the limited artefactual evidence, means that there is a definite dearth of "precise academic knowledge" regarding shields and their use, suggesting a lack of understanding with regard to other aspects of ancient Egyptian warfare and military equipment.[657] Stonborough's experiments, along with my 2009 and 2013 work, seek to address these issues and add to the understanding of ancient Egyptian warfare in general.[658]

Stonborough had the following research questions to address:

- How, and from what materials, were Old and Middle Kingdom infantry shields constructed?
- Were single sheets of rawhide really suitable for the construction of Middle Kingdom shields?
- How effective were these shields in combat?
- Did the introduction of new close-combat weaponry (such as the *khopesh*-sword) during the Second Intermediate Period make a change in shield materials necessary?[659]

Stonborough sought to address these research questions by manufacturing an infantry shield himself, based upon the type of shield widely used in the Middle Kingdom;[660] one that was made from a sheet of rawhide without a frame or a backing other than a crossbar.[661] The shield was then tested for its effectiveness and resilience, in controlled conditions, with the use of professionally manufactured replica weapons that were typically used in Egypt and the Near East in the New Kingdom period.[662]

With such little artefactual evidence for the shields used in the Middle Kingdom and New Kingdom, Stonborough's attempts at creating a replica shield had to incorporate a certain degree of inference, a series of educated estimates.[663] Along with this, the construction of a completely historically and archaeologically accurate replica requires tools, materials, means, and specialist skills somewhat beyond those which were available within the scope of the experiment at the time it was carried out.[664] As a result of this, Stonborough's intentions were not to create an exact replica, but to manufacture a close approximation of such an item using modern equipment, materials, and techniques for practical reasons.[665] Despite the use of modern techniques, Stonborough took great care with the design, construction, and selection of appropriate materials for the shield components in order to gain the most archaeologically useful/accurate results from the experiments.[666]

Looking at the materials used for the main body of the shield face, Stonborough used a single sheet of de-haired rawhide (modern EU regulations requiring any hides produced by British tanneries to pass through processes which mean that hide hairs are removed).[667] This de-haired hide differs from the (probably) haired rawhide used by the ancient Egyptians in the Middle Kingdom and New Kingdom; the density of the modern hide is less than that of the ancient equivalent and has greater flexibility. However, there are enough similarities for the modern rawhide to be a sensible and useful proxy/alternative to an exact replica.[668]

It has generally been agreed[669] that the dimensions of the shields in question (those most frequently used by soldiers from the Old and the Middle Kingdom), were a standard infantry shield about 1 m in height. Although there seems to have been larger shields, for reasons of practicality, and due to the increased frequency of their portrayal in ancient Egyptian art, Stonborough decided to reproduce one of the smaller shields for the experiment.[670]

As there is no surviving example of such a shield in the artefactual archaeological record, Stonborough acquired approximate measurements for the shields from non-artefactual sources, such as the highly detailed wooden models of spearmen from Mesehti's tomb. As ancient Egyptian tomb models often displayed a significant degree of realism,[671] Stonborough assumed that the craftsman who made the model spearmen attempted to produce models of real soldiers and their equipment roughly to scale.[672] He decided to apply this relationship to the replica shield, using his own height as a reference, in order to give himself as realistic an impression of the shape, weight, and handling of such a shield as possible preceding the testing of it against the replica weapons.[673]

Stonborough is at pains to point out that, whilst the dimensions of the entire Mesehti model regiment have been published, the dimensions of the individual figures have not, so the measurements for his replica shield were inferred from a photograph of the model. This resulted in estimated dimensions of a height of 90 cm and a width of 45 cm.[674] Stonborough accepted that there would be a reasonable margin of error given the less-than-accurate methods used, but noted that the shields used by ancient Egyptian soldiers would have been manufactured by hand and would probably have differed from each other to a certain degree in their dimensions.[675] He therefore decided that this margin of error would be acceptable within the designed framework of the experiment he was carrying out.[676]

When it came to the crossbar, it was again decided that a similar margin of error would be adopted, as the three crossbars displayed in the Metropolitan Museum of Art in New York had no measurement details, except for the crossbar with the accession number 27.3.70 (which had a length of 82 cm recorded for it).[677] This crossbar was therefore used as a template for the replica as rest of the dimensions could be inferred from the crossbar reference photograph in the online collection database of the Metropolitan Museum.[678] It was not deemed necessary for the replica crossbar to be an identical copy, to the millimetre, of the one in the Metropolitan Museum, for the same reasons as those applied to the rawhide shield-face. As the experiment in which the shield was to be tested did not involve actual person-to-person combat testing (for reasons of health and safety!), it was deemed that an absolute replica of the crossbar and handle was not necessary (which it would have been if it was to be used in a form of actual combat, as the shape and size of the handle would almost certainly have an effect on the shield's handling in such a situation).[679] For these experiments, the crossbar only needed to have approximately the same stability and resilience effect on the shield as the original in the Metropolitan Museum.[680] Therefore, Stonborough decided to assume that crossbar 27.3.70 was designed for an Egyptian shield, although it was likely made for a shield of a larger size than the regular infantry shield of the type held by Mesehti's spearmen.[681] As a result, Stonborough decided to keep the shape and measurements of 27.3.70 with regard to the manufacture of the replica crossbar, except for the crossbar length, which he shortened to 45 cm in order to match-up to the width of the experimental shield face.[682]

The online catalogue for the crossbar 27.3.70 does not indicate what type of wood it was composed of, which Stonborough mentions as presenting a problem, as different types of wood would have very different characteristics. The wood used for an ancient Egyptian (or any civilisation, for that matter) shield crossbar would have needed to be strong in order to withstand strikes from various types of weapons and would also need to be flexible enough to absorb significant amounts of kinetic energy without shattering.[683] For practical reasons, Stonborough decided to use common ash for the manufacture of his crossbar, as ash has high tensile strength and is suitably robust, apparently making it an appropriate substitute for whatever wood the ancient Egyptians would actually have used when manufacturing their own crossbars.[684]

When it came to manufacturing the shield face, Stonborough started by stretching dampened cowhide tightly over a wooden frame, measuring 150 x 110 cm, and fastening it to the frame with the use of steel nails (**Figure 5.36 – see plates**).[685] Shade-drying was often used in antiquity in order to dry hides and Stonborough sought to replicate the process in his experiment. The frame onto which the hide was stretched was kept under a covered and sheltered archway and was then left there for three days to dry and stiffen.[686] After the three days had passed, the frame and hide were completely warped due to the tension created by the hide shrinking as it dried (**Figure 5.37 – see plates**); there was just enough of a flat area left that could be used to manufacture the shield face, although it was not of uniform thickness. It was also not as thick as he had initially intended the shield face to be.[687] Stonborough then cut out a rectangle of approximately 45 x 90 cm using a heavy-duty steel cutter, something that seemingly required a great deal of strength and patience, as the hide was extremely tough[688] (boding well for its effectiveness against at least bladed weapons). Once the rectangle of hide was cut out, it was then shaped to resemble the forms of the shields held by Mesehti's soldiers, with a tapered tip starting approximately two-thirds of the way up the shield face.[689]

When it came to attaching the replica crossbar to the shield face, Stonborough pierced the hide with a series of holes, about two-thirds of the way up, that also corresponded to grooves made in the crossbar (**Figure 5.38 – see plates**). The crossbar was tightly tied to the back of the shield face with the use of jute string; the string had been coated in beeswax in order to reduce any friction or wear as the shield was used (**Figure 5.39 – see plates**).[690] Stonborough states that he did not use any form of adhesive (e.g. modern glue or glue of a similar composition to those used in antiquity), as there is apparently no clear evidence that any adhesive was used in ancient Egypt, nor was it possible to easily get hold of a suitably accurate glue such as one used in ancient Egypt.[691]

When it came to setting up the main aspect of the experiment (testing the effectiveness of the replica shield against weaponry), Stonborough made use of the same axe and *khopesh* that I used in the experiments discussed above. As such sharp and potentially dangerous weapons were to be used, Stonborough felt it prudent to not have the shield held by a human being.[692] The design of the experiment aimed to replicate, as safely and as accurately as possible, the circumstances under which the shield would have been used had it been held on a human arm in actual physical combat.[693] Therefore, he drilled a hole through the tip of the shield and hung it from a tree branch at the height at which he would have naturally held it in the same position as the shields were held by Mehseti's soldiers.[694] Three more holes were drilled along the bottom edge of the shield face; the holes were used to tie the shield to a heavy weight on the ground via the middle hole, with bungee cords hooked in the corner holes and tied to the ground on either side via the use of metal tent pegs (**Figure 5.40 – see plates**).[695] This set-up meant that the shield was held securely but could be effectively attacked along the face and sides without obstruction from the fastenings. The elasticity of the cords meant that there was a certain amount of 'give' to the set-up, replicating the way in which the shield would have provided resistance when wielded by a human being against a blow from a weapon.[696]

Stonborough has some interesting observations regarding the handling of the replica shield, particularly with regard to its effectiveness in active warfare:

> "The shield is very light, and easily carried in the same fashion as depicted on Mesehti's wooden soldiers. The shape of the crossbar by which it is held contributes to its overall stability, and protects the back of the hand which holds it. Due to the shape of its rounded, tapered top, the shield is very protective of the head and face, and blocking attacks to those areas from most angles requires very little movement and effort… In contrast to the good upper body protection conferred by this shield, blocking blows to the lower areas of the body, such as the legs, requires much more movement. Indeed, it is necessary either to crouch very low or to turn the shield upside-down completely in order to protect one's legs and knees, thus opening up the upper part of the body to attack. However, the lightness of the shield partly makes up for this relative lack of efficiency, as it enables the shield to be moved very quickly with minimal effort."[697]

When it came to testing out the actual weapons against the shield, the first set of blows were aimed at where the neck of the person holding the shield was presumed to have been located **(Figures 5.41 and 5.42 – see plates)**.[698] This particular aim was taken so as to test the strength of the shield rim against each of the weapons, the area of shield rim tested fortuitously being the thickest section of hide (the section right above the crossbar). Stonborough reckoned to have been the section most representative of the thickness of actual ancient Egyptian shields.[699]

The first strike against the shield rim was from the replica axe and was fascinating in the result it produced: "It left such a minimal trace of impact that it was initially assumed to have missed. A further two blows were then struck with the axe on the same spot, causing only a slight indentation and flattening of the shield edge"[700] **(Figure 5.43 – see plates)**. The next strike against the shield rim was from the replica *khopesh*. This was aimed at the same section but a little below where the axe had hit, in order to preserve the result created by the blow from the axe and to ensure that any blow from the *khopesh* would not be affected by the previous blows from the axe. This weapon had a very different, but equally fascinating, result to the blow from the axe: "The *khopesh* sliced effortlessly through 6.8 cm of the shield before stopping. It was considered unnecessary to deliver further blows to this edge with the *khopesh* after obtaining this result, as its capacity to cut cleanly through rawhide had been established beyond doubt"[701] **(Figure 5.44 – see plates)**.

After testing the effectiveness of the shield rim, Stonborough then moved onto testing the resilience of the surface of the shield face; striking once with the axe and once with the *khopesh*, aiming below the crossbar.[702] The results of these strikes were also very interesting: "The axe blow to the face of the shield created a c. 1 mm deep and 5.4 cm long scar (**Figure 5.45 – see plates**) at point of impact. The blow struck with the *khopesh* left the shield face mostly undamaged, apart from a long scratch on its surface. However, the tip of the *khopesh* did leave a scar similar to that left by the axe, though much smaller and less deep"[703] (**Figure 5.46 – see plates**).

Stonborough's analysis of the experiments provided insight into not only the performance of the shield, but also the performance of the *khopesh* and the axe. He points out that the negligible damage caused by the axe to the edge of the shield is most likely due to the fact that the specific shape of the axe-head (broad and wedge-shaped) meant that the impact was absorbed entirely by the shield edge.[704] In direct contrast to this, the much narrower *khopesh* blade produced a significantly smaller area of impact, cutting through the shield edge not only very easily, but to such a degree that it would have been possibly lethal (or at least dangerous and wounding) to the person wielding the shield in defence.[705]

The type and degree of damage caused by the two weapons seems to have been switched around when it came to the testing of the shield face: the "lighter, longer blade, whilst excellent for cutting, could not develop a sufficient force of impact to significantly damage the rawhide surface of the shield. The heavier axe-head proved far more effective in this respect, although it did not manage to penetrate the shield".[706] It is fascinating to see the results that Stonborough produced with his experiments; the effectiveness of the rawhide shield against the two different types of bladed weaponry, and the varied impacts the two weapons made on the shield, were particularly interesting when compared with the results from the experiments I carried out, both in 2009 and in 2014. The comparisons are helped by the consistency of the weapons used in the experiments. The variations seen in how the axe and *khopesh* impacted on the pig remains are reflected in the damage done to the shield: the heavier, crushing injuries seen in the pig X-rays caused by the axe are echoed in the lack of cutting action seen on the shield edge and the severe, slicing trauma seen on the pig remains after a blow from the *khopesh* is clearly demonstrated by the long slice through the shield rim.

As pointed out by Stonborough (and indeed earlier in this book), until swords became more popular in the New Kingdom, the axe, the mace, and the spear, were the close-combat weapons of preference for the ancient Egyptian infantry.[707] He suggests that such generally uncomplicated and easily-made weapons would have also been used by Egypt's neighbours and enemies; ancient Egyptian soldiers' personal defensive apparatus would have been developed and engineered as a direct result of this, in order to repel such weapons.[708] Stonborough's experiment quite clearly establishes that the rawhide shields could certainly "withstand shock loads delivered by weapons such as maces and axes, which rely on impact and penetration to cause damage".[709] Although Stonborough is at pains to point out that his experiments do not absolutely prove that ancient Egyptian shields were manufactured with exactly the methods shown in the experiment, it is important to note that the experiment and its results do, to some extent, validate Hayes' theory regarding shields, particularly in relation to the physical characteristics of the raw materials used in their construction.[710]

It is also worth noting that Stonborough has his reservations with regard to just how effective the sort of shield he manufactured would be against long and narrow slicing blades – a rawhide shield with no frame or any other sort of back would seem to leave its wielder somewhat vulnerable to a weapon such as a sword by the time of the New Kingdom, when swords were more widely used (such as the *khopesh*).[711] Stonborough suggests that the introduction of the *khopesh* and other sword types in the Second Intermediate Period may have made such a shield redundant (although, as pointed out in an earlier chapter in this book, there were forms of swords in the Middle Kingdom, different as they were to the *khopesh* swords seen in the New Kingdom). The changes in shape in shields from the New Kingdom onwards may well have been accompanied by other construction alterations, such as inclusion of wooden backings or frames that would reinforce the shields against the influx of cutting and slicing weapons.[712]

As has been pointed out by Stonborough himself, the rawhide used by the ancient Egyptians in the manufacture of these types of shields was probably denser and stiffer than that used in the 2011 experiment and would therefore have provided a more robust defence against attacks from bladed (and blunt-force) weapons.[713] The theory put forward by Stonborough is that had the experiment been repeated, but with a shade-dried hide that had not been de-haired, it could well have been the case that the *khopesh* would have caused less damage than it did in the actual experiment.[714] The ancient Egyptian hide shields may well have provided sufficient protection against close-combat weapons such as those introduced in the Second Intermediate Period (e.g. the *khopesh*). The alteration in shield design that was portrayed in New Kingdom artwork does, however, imply that the ancient Egyptians found it necessary to make some sort of modifications to shield design, perhaps in response to the new weapons the infantry faced from the Second Intermediate Period onwards.[715]

Future avenues of study (particularly with regard to experimental archaeology such as that carried out in 2011) could include not only improving on the manufacture of a rawhide shields, but also could examine the effectiveness of such a shield against other types of weaponry, such as spears, and projectiles, such as the compound bow and arrow. Until such experiments could be carried out it is impossible to speculate with certainty just how well a rawhide shield would hold up against these weapons.[716]

However, what Stonborough's experiment has shown is that a rawhide shield made from a single sheet of cowhide, such as the type held by Mehseti's soldiers, would have certainly provided an admirable level of defence against certain types of close-combat weaponry used in warfare in the Old and Middle Kingdoms.[717] On top of the defensive capabilities of the shield, the lightness and ease of handling of such a piece of equipment would have made the shield invaluable to the ancient Egyptian soldier on the move.[718]

Experimental Archaeology

These experiments demonstrate how certain ancient Egyptian weapons were used and just how effective they would have been. The aim of the experiments was also to prove definitively that the weapons studied could have served a functional purpose in combat, even when employed by women. While I am not arguing that women regularly participated in the military, evidence from the wall scene from Deshahsheh shows that women might have had to take up arms when their homes and lives were put under military threat.

This experimental archaeology has shown the effectiveness of the dagger, the axe, and the *khopesh* when wielded by both male and female test subjects and how women would have been more than capable of utilising the specific weaponry with great effect, even without formal training. This would probably have been the case with the women portrayed using daggers in the aforementioned scene from Deshasheh. Although the mace did not appear to be as effective as the other weapons, it is clear that it still could have been a lethal weapon.

It has been suggested that there is absolutely no evidence for ancient Egyptian women being involved in military activity at all.[719] This is certainly the case with regard to the official, structured ancient Egyptian military/army, but does not take into account examples such as female pharaohs or women defending themselves. Whilst it may seem obvious that a weapon such as the *khopesh* is a dangerous and indeed lethal instrument, it historically seems to have been regarded as having a purely symbolic purpose when held in the hands of a woman (i.e. the Nefertiti smiting scene). In contrast, the same weapon found in the same context but linked with a man is automatically regarded as functional. It has therefore been the case that certain weapons have been categorised as either votive or functional objects based solely on the gender of the individual it has been related to.

The mace[720] is particularly interesting as it is likely to have played both a functional and a symbolic role, especially in smiting scenes. The mace held by Hatshepsut on the obelisk depiction is employed as a symbol of her power (as is the example of Neferure, Hatshepsut's daughter, discussed in an earlier chapter) while actual examples, such as the huge Scorpion mace-head, can be described as purely ceremonial. Others, such as the maces found in the Predynastic burials, are most likely to be functional weapons; the chipped edges of many providing evidence of their active use.

The experiments designed for this book deal specifically with the weapons associated with women in ancient Egypt, whether in artistic portrayals or weapons found in female burials. However, the results also have relevance when looking at ancient Egyptian weapons in general. The mace had already been shown to be an effective weapon in my previous research,[721] based on experiments I carried out using the pigs' heads as a human proxy. Although the subsequent mace experiments demonstrated that the mace was less effective in damaging sections of pig ribcage, invaluable information was nonetheless obtained on how this particular weapon would be best employed against a human being. They also demonstrated the effectiveness of the mace as a weapon, no matter what the biological sex of the person wielding it.

As with the discussion of women involved in warfare, defensive equipment has not been studied as rigorously as other aspects of Egyptian archaeology.[722] Many theories have been put forward but little has been done to make any moves towards proving, or at least supporting, them[723] and what research has been done has not addressed most of the issues with the current state of knowledge on the nature of Egyptian defensive military apparatus.[724] Stonborough's experiments have done a great deal to rectify this but he is clear about the limitations of his work. Overall, there is a great deal more to be done on the subject.

One area which could provide a wider range of evidence is the examination of mummified remains beyond Egypt. In most cases the examination of such bodies tends to concentrate on embalming techniques, with any evidence of trauma considered as almost an afterthought; some previously examined bodies have only recently been identified as having any form of trauma at all. Currently there are just a few examples of mummies displaying evidence of weapons trauma and it could well be that there are several more potential mummies with such trauma out there, just waiting for investigation and analysis.

The experiments presented here have been very illuminating when it comes to examining aspects of offensive and defensive warfare in Dynastic Egypt. Each experiment on its own has proven to be fascinating and, when taking the experiments and their results together, a great deal is revealed about the nature of weaponry used and the methods chosen to defend against attacks from such weapons. Experimental archaeology of this kind helps to move the discipline forwards, and in some cases, challenges long-held assumptions about prescribed gender roles, allowing a more rounded and nuanced view of life in ancient Egypt.

6

Weapons Trauma in Ancient Egypt

When looking at weapons trauma in ancient Egyptian remains, it is important to remember that people killed in battle were rarely mummified intentionally. As such, examples of injuries sustained in battle are rarely to be found in the mummies which have been examined historically. The majority of the wounds which have been seen are head wounds making it somewhat difficult to draw too many comparisons with the experimental archaeology I have carried out here. Nonetheless, this evidence does exist and it bears a closer examination if we are to look closely at ancient Egyptian warfare.

The Slain Soldiers of Montu-hotep

Discovered in 1923, the Slain Soldiers of Montu-hotep provide one of the most extensive sources of evidence for weapons trauma in ancient Egyptian remains. This group of soldiers are believed to have been killed in battle and then buried near the temple of Montu-hotep at Deir el-Bahri.[725] The bodies of the Slain Soldiers had never been placed in coffins, only wrapped in linen and simply placed one on top of the other. This meant that the bodies in this mass grave became contorted over time as they were not laid out evenly.[726] As a result, there were only ten cases in which complete bodies have been found.[727]

A number of these soldiers had evidence of old and long-healed wounds from previous conflicts, which suggests that they were experienced warriors and veterans of at least one previous battle. The injuries, although showing signs of healing, seem to have been serious ones, including a couple of examples of what appears to be blunt-force trauma. In his work on these soldiers, Winlock describes one man's skull as having potential mace damage while another has an oval-shaped dent visible on it.[728] I would definitely suggest that this trauma could have been caused by a blow from a mace. The size of the depression is not dissimilar to the approximate size of some of the globular maces in use at that time. It is also possible that these injuries were caused by rocks being thrown at the heads of the soldiers[729] but without further study it is impossible to confirm absolutely either way.[730]

At least eighteen substantial peri-mortem head injuries can be found on these soldiers which have been thought to be a result of missiles, such as rocks, being thrown down on them.[731] One soldier displayed a large cut in his scalp (measuring 6 cm long by 1 cm wide) which cut right through to the surface of his right frontal bone.[732] Winlock sticks with the theory that rocks and stones caused these injuries,[733] but it has also been suggested (and not just by me) that a mace or a stave could be held responsible for this trauma.[734] These sorts of wounds were not always fatal, but they would at the very least have been disabling, potentially causing unconsciousness the instant the blow made contact with the skull.[735]

Stones or maces were not the only dangers faced by these soldiers, some of their remains display what could possibly be axe damage. Winlock describes the injuries sustained in gleefully graphic detail, recounting how one soldier's face (body HH) had been crushed from the left-hand side with huge sections of the facial structure being completely obliterated, the bone fragments still stained with blood even several thousand years later.[736] This damage suggests that the attacker was likely right-handed and wielded his weapon with considerable strength.[737] The description of the trauma suggests to me that the axe is a definite candidate for causing these injuries. As discovered during the experimental archaeology discussed in the previous chapter, the axe was useful as both a cutting and clubbing weapon. The crushing and shattering of the facial bones could indicate a clubbing action as being the primary cause of injury, whilst the copious blood staining would indicate that soft tissue and underlying blood vessels would have been slashed. An axe such as the Eighteenth Dynasty one I used could definitely be capable of causing such trauma (you only need to look at the photos and X-Rays of the axe experiments to see that).

Another example that shows possible axe damage is body KK, which also had the left-side of the face crushed, with the nose and lower orbit bones pushed to the right-had side (again suggesting a right-handed opponent).[738] The fractured surfaces were stained with the soldier's blood meaning that the damage on body KK could be consistent with a blow to the head by an axe or even from a conical mace, particularly if it had a very sharp edge.[739] My 2009 experiments showed that the conical mace-head edge could split skin and break bone in a pig's head, so it is easy enough to theorise that the damage caused to a human skull by the same weapon would be more extensive.[740] It has also been suggested that some of the wounds were inflicted post-mortem (a way for the attackers to make sure their opponents were definitely dead),[741] although the blood stains on the bones would imply that at least the main blow was peri-mortem.

The *Slain Soldiers* certainly display various weapon wounds from active combat making them worthy of discussion, but they are a rare occurrence as large groups of wounded mummified bodies are not a common find in Egypt.[742] They are a very useful source with which to study ancient Egyptian weapons trauma but, beyond Winlock's and McDermott's works,[743] there is not an awful lot else that has been done on them. Most other work is usually a repetition of Winlock's original book with little attempt to analyse the remains any further. There is a huge potential for future work that could be done, involving a more in-depth analysis of the remains, with better quality photographs.[744] This all depends on whether the remains are in a decent enough condition for further study, of course, something that is perhaps in doubt, but it is an interesting avenue of future study nonetheless.

These bodies are useful to look at because they tell us so much about the possible weapons that were used in this period. The fact that some the wounds could possibly be attributed to mace damage is interesting as it would suggest that the mace was, at times, used more in battle than we have previously thought. What we can learn from this is that it is possible that the mace had uses beyond just being a ceremonial/execution weapon

The Royal Mummy of Seqenenre

Not all known weapons trauma have been found on the remains of professional soldiers, some can be seen on the remains of individual mummies. One such example is the mummified body of Seqenenre (Seqenenra, Saqnounri) Tao II, a pharaoh from the end of the Second Intermediate Period Seventeenth Dynasty.[745] Seqenenre also has a very interesting connection with something discussed earlier in this book as he was the husband of Queen Ahhotep, the queen who led troops into battle against the Hyksos and who obviously did a lot better out of the whole warfare thing than her husband did, as we shall see.

The mummy of Seqenenre was found in 1881 in a cache of royal bodies buried in Tomb DB.320 at Deir el-Bahri.[746] Seqenenre was a Theban ruler, who started the series of campaigns against the Hyksos that eventually led to them being expelled from Egypt by Ahhotep and Ahmose I, Seqenenre's son.[747] Taken to the Cairo Museum, Seqenenre's mummy was unwrapped by Gaston Maspero (1886) and examined by the anatomist Grafton Elliot Smith.[748] Whilst Smith bemoans the damaged state of the mummy, he does point out that the body was not in the traditional pose chosen for mummified pharaohs. Instead, the body had not been straightened and the arms and hands were left extended and twisted as if the pharaoh had died in agony, his hands twisted with the pain.[749]

Admittedly, Smith's description is perhaps a tad overly-dramatic; but it does demonstrate the state of the body before what is likely to have been a minimal and quick battlefield mummification.[750] The general style of the mummification of Seqenenre was one that was in use at the end of the Seventeenth Dynasty and the beginning of the Eighteenth Dynasty, but was in this case carried out in a hasty manner.[751] This is certainly indicative of a hurried battlefield mummification, especially as the brain was still left inside the head, contrary to the mummification customs of the time.[752]

It has been suggested that Seqenenre died on the battlefield but was not immediately mummified in an emergency procedure, instead being transported back to Thebes for mummification.[753] It is possible that the days the corpse spent travelling in hot temperatures affected it quite badly, leaving it in a state of decomposition by the time the embalmers received it.[754] Yet Smith quickly dismisses this in favour of Maspero's theory of a battlefield embalming; if the body had in fact been taken to embalmers in Thebes for a proper mummification, they surely would have laid it out in a traditional pose and would not embalm it as hastily as they appear to have done.[755]

What is of main interest to me, though, is the evidence of trauma on the pharaoh's remains. Firstly, there is a distinctive wound on the frontal bone, running 63 mm across from the middle line to the right-hand side of the skull.[756] It is mentioned that the scalp was cut by this blow, with the edges of the scalp wound apparently suggesting that the weapon hit when Seqenenre was still alive.[757] This theory is also backed-up by the fact that to the right of this wound is a blood-soaked crescent-shaped mass of hair.[758] The presence of blood directly related to the wound would seem to indicate that it was likely to have been inflicted peri-mortem.[759]

Seqenenre looks to have been injured more than once as there was also a crack in the skull, which was a result of the fracture created by an arrow wound.[760] Along this crack, there was a patch of bare bone that is thought to have been caused either by a blow from another weapon or from a projection on the weapon used to create the original wound.[761] Smith put forward that this particular wound (and all the resulting damage) was caused by an axe[762] and I quite agree with him. The possible dimensions of the axe edge are extrapolated from the wound, with the measurements being estimated at 5-6 cm long.[763] The damage to the scalp, along with the fracturing and cracking of the bone, would seem to corroborate this, especially when compared to the soft tissue and bone damage that was inflicted by the axe when tested in the experimental archaeology I carried out.[764] The time period, and the calculated dimensions of the axe edge, would indicate that the type of axe used to create this particular wound is of a similar type to the replica used to carry out my experiments. Certainly, some forensic examination of Seqenenre's mummy in the 1970s also indicated a match between the wounds on Seqenenre's head and the style of Palestinian axe-head from that era.[765] This would seem to corroborate the theory that Seqenenre did in fact die in combat against the Hyksos rulers.[766]

If that was not enough, Seqenenre also suffered another head wound which can be found below the blood-soaked hair. This time it is a fusiform wound (wide in the middle and tapered at either end) on the scalp, which shows another coextensive frontal bone fracture, 31 mm long.[767] This wound was possibly caused by an axe[768] but it does bear a significant resemblance to the damage done to the pig skull by a conical mace during my experiments.[769] However, at this stage it is hard to be conclusive as it can be difficult to distinguish between all the wounds on the head especially since there are several of them.[770]

Yet another wound can be found across Seqenenre's nose which fractured both of his nasal bones and also seems to have destroyed his right eye.[771] Due to the nature of the injury, it is difficult to determine what it was caused by but it could have been a stick, an axe handle, a club, or even a mace.[772] There is also another possible axe wound on the left cheek, cutting through the skin and severing the malar from the superior maxilla.[773]

The unfortunate Seqenenre did not just suffer blunt-force trauma, but also what seems to be sharp-force trauma from a pointed weapon (such as a metal spear or dagger) which entered his body below the ear on the left side of his head.[774] The generally accepted theory is that this wound was caused by a dagger, which would be in-keeping with the weapon designs of the era.[775] Whichever weapon was used, it caused a debilitating and, quite probably, fatal injury.[776]

It is obvious that Seqenenre died a rather violent death. The evidence of extensive trauma to the head but no injuries on the arm, torso, or any other parts of the body, potentially suggest that Seqenenre did not fight back against his attackers.[777] It has been suggested that the wounds were inflicted whilst Seqenenre was lying on his right-hand side, perhaps asleep, which would go some way to explaining why there were no defensive injuries.[778]

The exact location of his wounds would back-up the theory that Seqenenre was attacked whilst lying down.[779] It is unlikely for a man of his height (1.70m) to have taken two horizontal wounds to the top of his head, from both the left side and from the front, had he been standing up.[780] Even if Seqenenre had been attacked a man of similar height or taller (or by a man on horseback) the blows would probably have been vertical, resulting in corresponding vertical wounds.[781] While this could indicate that Seqenenre was killed whilst napping on the job, it is also the possible that Seqenenre was first felled by a blow from a spear, after which he lay on the ground unconscious whilst the rest of the blows were inflicted.[782]

There is another, altogether more intriguing, theory of Seqenenre's death: that he was assassinated.[783] Winlock argues that the way in which Seqenenre's body was positioned post-mortem shows how those who prepared him did not wish for him to be buried with all necessary pharaonic honours, possibly suggesting a hasty disposal of an assassination victim.[784] A slightly more likely explanation, however, is that Seqenenre actually died as a result of a ceremonial execution carried out by a Hyksos commander upon the Theban's battlefield defeat.[785] This conclusion was apparently reached through a combination of physical, textual, and statistical evidence: re-examining Maspero's original unwrapping of the mummy, recent analysis by medical experts, and some experimental archaeology.[786]

Whichever theory you prefer, it is very obvious that Seqenenre died a violent death, with injuries inflicted by multiple weapons and quite possibly multiple assailants.[787] The evidence which I am most interested in here is the clear weapons trauma on Seqenenre's body, which is extremely useful for comparison with the experimental archaeology I have carried out.[788] It is important to examine examples of weapons trauma such as this, for we can learn so much about the development of the weapons used in this period and we can also learn a great deal directly about the possible causes of death of a pharaoh. This is an example when we do not have to rely on textual or artistic references for the demise of the pharaoh, as we can look at the pharaoh himself and make our judgements from there. Comparing it to the damage seen in my experiment shows whether or not we were using accurate replicas and techniques for testing out the weaponry.

Lesser Known Remains

There are a number of other examples of weapons injuries which have been found in ancient Egyptian remains. Whilst they may not be as spectacular or as well-documented as the *Slain Soldiers* or the mummy of Seqenenre, they are nevertheless informative and relevant to the work done in the book.

Dra Abu el Naga

Found at Dra Abu el Naga, on the west bank of the Nile, is a possible case of homicide in an Egyptian mummy head.[789] The mummy head was found in tomb K93.11 and has been dated to the late Egyptian period (between Twenty-Second and Twenty-Sixth dynasties).[790] The head was identified as being from as a male individual, of around 20-40 years old.[791]

When archaeologists examined these remains, it was found that there is a rounded depression in the skin over the left posterior skull and a small irregular crescentic skin defect.[792] The soft tissue around the wound had turned brown but was still intact.[793] Once the soft tissue was removed, there was an obvious rounded hole in the underlying skull, something that is typical in depressed skull fractures of this kind.[794] There were no other defects present in the skull, nor were there any defects observable on the preserved right-side of the face. In addition to removing the soft tissue from the damaged area, a radiological examination of the damage exposed a secondary fracture running at a right-angle from the hole.[795]

The brown colouring of the soft tissue could well be as a result of bleeding, which would support the view that this particular damage was either peri-mortem or very early post-mortem.[796] I would personally agree with idea of this wound being inflicted just before death, probably causing his death itself. As with one of the theories applied to Seqenenre, the suggestion is also that this unknown male was attacked with a powerful blow from a rounded weapon whilst he was lying on the ground.[797] Such a blow would have at the very least caused unconsciousness, if not death.[798]

It is likely that this trauma was caused by a weapon such as a mace or a club.[799] The injury certainly seemed to be indicative of blunt-force trauma, reflecting a blow from a mace or club, or even a rock (perhaps being used as a weapon of opportunity).[800] Whilst this example cannot be directly compared to the trauma demonstrated by the experimental archaeology I have carried out here, it is nevertheless an interesting example of the possible impact of blunt force trauma on an ancient Egyptian skull and is perhaps more comparable with the results seen in the experimental archaeology I carried out in 2009. The trauma caused by the globular mace-head in 2009 is similar to some extent to the damage seen here, but without pig-skull from the globular mace-head experiment (which is presumably languishing in a fox den somewhere in Heslington) it is impossible to make the direct comparison I would want to. This certainly calls for further research and experimentation in the future.

Giza

One other Late Period example I want to look at comes from Giza, dated from the Twenty-Sixth to the Thirtieth Dynasties. This was a site that was excavated by Petrie where he found a staggering 1,726 skulls, 21 of which displayed evidence of head injuries (1.2%).[801] In these skulls, the most common type of injury was a severe long and deep cut. There were five skulls that displayed this type of cut; four of the skulls being male, with the cuts suggested to have been caused by axes or swords being brought down forcefully on top of the head.[802] From my perspective the most interesting thing is that the fifth skull displaying this type of trauma is that of a female.[803] In contrast to the male skulls, the theory put forward here is that this particular trauma occurred due to a domestic dispute.[804] This seems to be an odd theory to apply to this example, considering the context of the skull finds. If the male skulls gained their trauma during military action, why should the reason for the female skull damage be any different? It is certainly possible for women to become involved in military or combat situations, even if they are not directly connected to the fighting. Gender is rarely taken into account in warfare and it is just as likely that women would be injured or killed as a result of military action as male non-combatants. As discussed previously in this book, this has been a continuing problem in archaeology and Egyptian archaeology in particular.

Three more of the skulls from Giza had regularly-shaped piercings that went right through the skull. This was almost certainly the cause of death, particularly as the hole showed no signs of healing (if not the direct cause of death, they were at least peri-mortem).[805] The theory is that these wounds were caused by spears[806] (again, another potential path for future experimental archaeology to take). One skull from the same site also displayed possible signs of depression trauma (similar to those seen on the *Slain Soldiers*), possibly sustained from an attack by a rock, club, or mace.[807] There were also other skulls that had linear cut injuries that were consistent with sword damage (although what type of sword exactly - straight or curved - is not specified) and at least one that had nicks consistent with the type of damage done by daggers or knives.[808]

What is apparent from these skull injuries is that most of them appear to have been sustained during a close-contact attack. There is no indication whether or not the remains were those of soldiers and it is possible that they were in fact civilians who were caught up in some form of warfare, possibly an attack on their settlement. The wide-ranging head injuries definitely suggest at least some military involvement and the weapons used were possibly made of iron (a more durable metal which was more readily available during the Late Dynastic Period) or bronze (which was still popular at this time).[809]

Torticollis

Moving forwards in time, there is a very interesting Graeco-Roman period mummy held at the Birmingham Museum and Art Gallery.[810] Dated to c. 300AD, the mummy has been identified as a male high-ranking soldier, tentatively aged at 25-35 years old at his death.[811] What is most interesting about this mummy is the injury he has sustained at some stage; when he was X-Rayed, the scans revealed a definite torticollis (a twisting of the neck muscles that would have kept the head twisted to one side[812]) to the right, with no evidence of arthritis seen in any of the joints.[813] This is relevant because of what else the X-Rays revealed: an arrowhead lodged in the right infratemporal fossa[814] (an area in the skull between the cheek bone and the jaw bone). The bronze or iron arrow-head had completely penetrated the soft tissue.[815] The belief is that the wound from this arrow caused an infection that resulted in muscle spasms responsible for the torticollis; this means that the soldier must have survived for at least some time after the initial wounding, the infection probably leading to his death[816]. Once rigor mortis had set in, it would have been near-impossible for the neck to be straightened during mummification.[817]

This example of ancient Egyptian trauma is really very interesting because it shows not just the immediate result of a wound from an arrow, but also the possible damage that can develop as a result of such an injury, where infection has possibly set in. The mummy has remained wrapped and has so far only been X-rayed so it is not possible to examine in detail the damage sustained by the soft tissue.[818] Whilst it is only conjecture that the arrow wound caused the torticollis (and it is indeed possible that there is some other idiopathic cause behind it), the X-Rays do provide evidence for the extent of the torticollis and the penetration of the arrowhead, which could potentially provide a useful resource for examining the long-lasting effect of combat on the health of those involved.[819]

Bahriyah Oasis

One final example also comes from the Graeco-Roman era and is from the Bahriyah Oasis, located in the Libyan Desert, 360 km southwest of Cairo.[820] Out of the 160 well-preserved adult skulls, thirty-one of them (belonging to both males and females) had some evidence of ante-mortem trauma.[821] One thing that I found particularly interesting here is that the investigators did not see the difference in ante-mortem trauma between the two sexes as being statistically significant.[822] The only mention of gender roles comes from the fact that some the fractures seen in some skulls may have been related to the environment in which the individuals existed; for example the role of carrying of water in large vessels is a typically female one and may account for the apparently higher frequency of cranial trauma in older adult females from the site.[823]

The weapons trauma evidence from this site ranged from depressed fractures to blade injuries, with the implication being that the depressed fractures were inflicted by blunt-force weaponry (potentially a piriform/globular mace or a club) and the sharp-force injuries were caused by some sort of edged weapons (such as a sword or an axe).[824] The size of the depressed fractures ranged from 20 mm to 56 mm in length, whereas the sharp-force trauma ranged from 19 mm to 86 mm;[825] definitely in keeping with maces for the fractures and axes or swords for the cuts.[826]

The apparently high rate of cranial trauma at the Bahriyah Oasis (in relation to other ancient Egyptian population groups at least) is quite possibly due to the Roman imperialism of the time: the rise of the Roman Empire (which included the Romans taking control of Egypt in this period) changed social and political relationship in Egypt.[827] This could well have created a climate of violence and caused conflict in some areas; the use of force is often central to ancient empire expansion.[828] Certainly, some of the cranial trauma could have been gained from face-to-face fighting, particularly the skulls that had injuries to the left-hand side of the face.[829] In contrast to this, the crania that had injuries to the back of the head were most likely people who had been hit with weaponry from behind whilst they were running away from their attackers.[830] It would suggest that the remains from Bahriyah were injured as a result of violence due to Roman imperial expansion, particularly when compared with the examples of the *Slain Soldiers* where the left-side fractures on the bodies were also interpreted as battle injuries.[831] This is, however, just one possible reason behind the trauma uncovered at Bahriyah and the remains will always be open to interpretation, both by archaeologists and other scientists. The potential for medical and archaeological study in the future with these sorts of remains is huge and there is always scope for further study.

Looking at Weapons Trauma

As mentioned above, the majority of examples of weapons trauma do appear to involve the skull and there is little work available on the equivalent damage to other parts of the body, such as the ribcage. Whilst this does pose some problems for direct comparison with the experimental archaeology I carried out (both in 2009 and 2012) the examples presented above are nevertheless extremely useful for the examination of weapons trauma. The injuries apparent on Seqenenre in particular are fascinating in relation to this, with multiple types of weapons trauma seen on his skull, some of which correspond to the trauma produced in my experimental archaeology.[832] These comparative examples also show the potential for future work that could be carried out within this subject. For instance, it would be an interesting option to test out multiple-era, period-accurate weapons on a suitable human head proxy (such as a sheep skull or an anatomically correct model), complete with digital modelling, to gain insight into exactly which weapons were used and exactly what impact they would have had beyond what can be seen visually alone.

Whilst this chapter deals with physical comparisons between the experimental archaeology I have carried out and the archaeological examples of trauma on ancient Egyptian remains, it has also raised some very serious points with regard to how such examples are interpreted by the academics studying them. Some examples have shown the problems within archaeology when there is a lack of gender or feminist-based approaches to the subject, particularly in relation to an archaeological examination of sexual difference within an ancient culture. Making sure that any interpretations are as accurate as possible (given the limitations of archaeological knowledge) is crucial in deepening our understanding of ancient Egyptian warfare and weaponry in general; not just in relation to gender in the ancient world.

Conclusion

An early line in this book stated that: "There can be no doubt that warfare in ancient Egypt is a well-studied subject". While this is inescapably true, it is my hope that throughout this book you have been introduced to aspects of warfare in ancient Egypt which have been largely overlooked in previous studies.

Using experimental archaeology we have been able to examine the capabilities of the various weapons shown in contemporary accounts and prove the effectiveness of such weapons when wielded by both male and female participants. The impressive results from the *khopesh* experiments in particular established the abilities of this weapon, even when employed by a person lacking in combat training. The evidence from the *Slain Soldiers* and the mummy of Seqenenre, along with the remains from Giza and the Bahriyah Oasis, proved to be very interesting; highlighting the exact nature of the damage individuals would have sustained in combat.

The occasional participation of women in warfare has sometimes been viewed as a novelty occurrence or quickly dismissed as an example of myth or folklore. It has been interpreted as being purely symbolic, an exaggeration in order to demonstrate political power. All too often, scholars and academics in the past (and sometimes even in current research) were influenced by outdated Nineteenth and Twentieth century Westernised attitudes towards the place of women in society, resulting in biased, inaccurate readings and interpretations of women throughout history. This is something that has been very much in evidence in past interpretations within Egyptian archaeology, particularly in relation to women in positions of power.

While there is no evidence that the majority of women played a fundamental or regular role in the military, it is clear that on occasion there is evidence for women using weapons or being actively involved in warfare in ancient Egypt. As we have seen, without any training women would have been able to wield ancient Egyptian weapons effectively. It is likely that most women who became involved in warfare took up arms with a view to defending their homes, lives, and families. Throughout history women have needed to defend themselves from attack whilst their menfolk were from home, yet this is rarely taken into consideration by many scholars who tend to focus on individual battles or campaigns. Even so, the evidence suggests that there were also a number of formidable women who were given (or took) greater power, using weapons during combat or executions and maintaining their status through a traditionally masculine display of power.

We have evidence focusing on some of the key women who wielded military and political power within Dynastic Egyptian society, although further research into the royal women would certainly enhance our knowledge of their roles within Egyptian society and its attitudes towards women in general. As a whole Dynastic Egypt could be described as generally having a patriarchal society, though research has shown that it was not impossible for women to hold the same roles as men (including the role of pharaoh).[833]

It is clear that more research needs to be done exploring the various images and interpretations that have been made with regard to prominent women in ancient Egypt, specifically taking into account the social and personal contexts and biases of previous archaeologists and biographers (for example, the work of Amelia Edwards). To critique earlier research in the simple terms of 'men underrating women' is too simplistic, we need to examine the more subtle historical and social influences in play. This is when a detailed feminist and gender-based approach to the subject can provide the best possible answers to many of the queries surrounding gender, biological sex, and the role of women in ancient Egypt.

So is any of this of interest beyond Egyptian archaeology?

Hopefully I have raised some interesting gender-based issues throughout this book, some of which have not gone away (especially not in Egyptian archaeology). A more rounded approach, which seeks to base interpretations on the evidence rather than on modern gender biases, is something that could be used in other areas of archaeology. In terms of the present learning from the past, re-investigating some of our assumptions about earlier societies may also be highly beneficial. As well as trying to counteract the idea of universal gender roles, we have seen the need for further research to be done on weapons trauma in mummies (both from Egypt and further abroad). Such examinations could help shed light on the range of weapons available in ancient societies, as well as the nature of the damage they could have caused.

Overall, I believe that there is definite potential for fruitful future research within this same subject area and beyond; the examination of weapons trauma on ancient mummified remains perhaps the most potentially valuable of all. With this book I hope to have given you a better understanding of the nature of women utilising weaponry in ancient Egypt, the attitudes toward women involved in warfare, and, to some extent, gender and feminist issues surrounding Egyptian archaeology as a whole.

I will have succeeded if this book has both informed and entertained at the same time. I have always believed that Archaeology does not have to be boring, especially not Military Archaeology where so many exciting things are studied. I can only hope that you have enjoyed reading about Egyptian warfare and weaponry as much I have studying it for the last seven years.

Appendix:
Harrogate Museums and Arts Collection

When it comes to looking at specific examples of the weapons used by the ancient Egyptians, it is best to examine artefacts directly and in person. I have been lucky enough to carry out a catalogue of certain weaponry artefacts in the Harrogate Museums and Arts.

Harrogate Museum has very kindly granted permission for me to use examples from their collections in this book. For all images, please see **Plates.**

The catalogue of weaponry held in the Harrogate Museums and Arts collection consists of eighteen artefacts, including the eight mace-heads I previously catalogued (2009). The 2009 cataloguing process was carried out in conjunction with a fellow student cataloguing some of the ancient Egyptian collections in North Yorkshire.[834] Therefore the artefacts have two 'Item/Catalogue Numbers': one assigned by Carolyn Gaunt and I (e.g. HAR1) and the one assigned by the museum (e.g. [10495]).

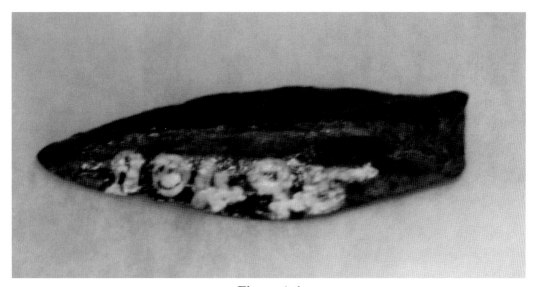

Figure A.1

Figure A.1 Bronze trilobate arrowhead of no recorded date, provenance or method of acquisition. The arrowhead is 36.3 mm in length, 11 mm in width (at the widest point) and a weight of 1 g. There is evidence of loop attachment. The arrowhead could possibly be from the Saite site of Defenneh, as it bears a very close resemblance to the types of arrowhead found during excavations by W.M. Flinders Petrie at Defenneh in 1886.

Figure A.2

Figure A.2 Bronze trilobate arrowhead with no recorded date, provenance or method of acquisition. The arrowhead is 41.25 mm in length, 14.67 mm in width (at the widest point) and has a weight of 5 g. As with the previous arrowhead (HAR1 [10495]), there is evidence of loop attachment and again this arrowhead could possibly be from the Saite site of Defenneh.

Figure A.3

Figure A.3 Bronze leaf-shaped spearhead with no recorded date, provenance or method of acquisition. The spearhead is 198.5 mm in length, 32.7 mm in width (at the widest point) and has a weight of 83 g. The spearhead has what is a possible hook attachment, which may have been used to attach it to a wooden shaft. The spearhead is in generally good condition although there is a large chip on one of the blade edges.

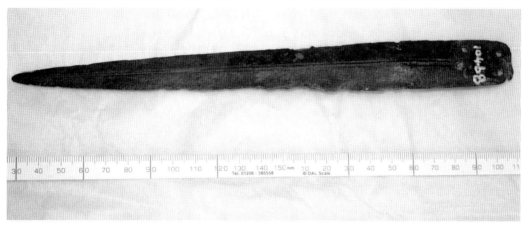

Figure A.4

Figure A.4 Bronze tapered spearhead with no recorded date, provenance or method of acquisition. The spearhead is 233 mm in length, 24.83 mm in width (at the widest point) and has a weight of 95 g. There is evidence of the use of bronze nails for attachment to a shaft, with four holes in total and a bronze nail remaining in one hole. It is uncertain as to whether the spear would have been thrown or thrust.

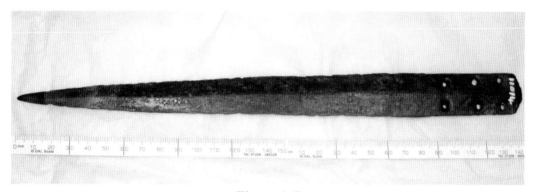

Figure A.5

Figure A.5 Bronze tapered spearhead with no recorded date, provenance or method of acquisition. The spearhead is 296.5 mm in length, 25.96 mm in width (at the widest point) and has a weight of 115 g. As with the previous spearhead (HAR4 [10468]), there is evidence of bronze nails for attaching the spearhead to the shaft with six point holes for attachment rather than four. It is possible that this spearhead has the same provenance as the previous one (HAR4 [10468]), though there are no provenance records for either of them. The spearhead is in relatively good condition with no warping at the tapered end. There are only a few chips present and the damage to the blade is limited. There appears to be some evidence of conservation and/or cleaning at the tapered end of the weapon. As with the previous spearhead

(HAR4 [10468]), it is uncertain as to whether the spear would have been thrown or thrust.

Figure A.6 Stone axe-head with no recorded date but a recorded provenance of Thebes in Egypt. The method of acquisition is listed as having come from the Kent Collection of artefacts bequeathed to the Museum in 1968 by B. W. J. Kent and given in 1969 to Harrogate Corporation.[835] The axe-head is 102.93 mm in length, 45.78 mm in width (at the widest point) and weighs 180 g. The axe-head still carries Kent's original label, stating the provenance and its item number from when it was part of that collection (423).

Figure A.6

Figure A.7 Stone axe-head with no recorded date. As with the previous axe-head (HAR12 [10434]), the recorded provenance is Thebes in Egypt and the method of acquisition is listed as having come from the Kent Collection. The axe-head is 115.59 mm in length, 47.15 mm in width (at the widest point) and weighs 195 g. As with the previous axe-head (HAR12 [10434]), it still carries Kent's original label, stating the provenance and its item number from when it was part of that collection (421).

Figure A.7

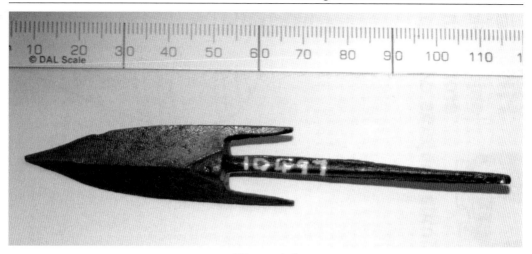

Figure A.8

Figure A.8 Bronze arrowhead or small spearhead with no recorded date, provenance or method of acquisition. The arrowhead/spearhead is 108.8 mm in length, 17.5 mm in width (at the widest point) and weighs 30 g. The arrowhead/spearhead is in generally good condition, although there is a small chip on one of the edges. There is also a small indistinct engraving on one side, perhaps a hieroglyph or some other symbol.

Figure A.9

Figure A.9 Bronze arrowhead with no date, provenance or method of acquisition. The arrowhead/spearhead is 143.7 mm in length, 22.5 mm in width (at the widest point) and has a weight of 20 g. The arrowhead is in excellent condition.

As the mace-heads have been previously catalogued (in 2007 and 2009),[836] they will be referred to in relation to those catalogues. All mace-heads were part of the collection bequeathed to the Museum in 1969, by the B. W. J. Kent collection,[837] unless otherwise stated.

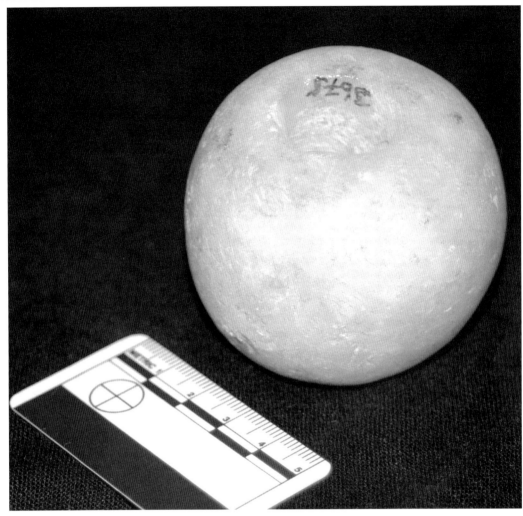

Figure A.10

Figure A.10 Predynastic piriform mace-head with no specific date recorded.[838] It is described in the museum records as being composed of light-coloured quartz, purported to be from Abydos, and had probably been ground down using an abrasive.[839] The mace-head is 54.49 mm in height, 57.45 mm in width (at the widest point) and weighs 300 g.[840] The central piercing of the mace-head was "drilled from [both] ends (probably using a bow drill), with the holes drilled aslant, missing the centre, and only meeting towards one of the ends".[841] The drilling error aside, this mace-head is in relatively good condition and is currently on display in the Royal Pump Room Museum in Harrogate.[842]

Figure A.11

Figure A.11 Predynastic globular mace-head, described in the museum records as being composed of dark brown diorite.[843] Again there is no specific date recorded, although the provenance is given as Abydos; the mace-head is 38.80 mm in height, 55.20 mm in width (at the widest point) and weighs 200 g.[844] The mace-head was most likely ground down using an abrasive, with a large central piercing drilled using a bow drill.[845] It is in extremely good condition and currently on display in the Royal Pump Room Museum in Harrogate.[846]

Figure A.12 Conical mace-head, described in the museum records as being composed of black porphyry with white crystals.[847] The mace-head is described as Predynastic and has been dated to c. 3200 B.C.E.[848] It is 38.80 mm in height, 55.20 mm in width (at the widest point) and weighs 200 g; it has a well drilled central piercing and is in good condition: "there are some chips and breaks on the edges, but these are negligible compared to the damage sustained by other mace-heads (such as mace-head 10549)".[849] This mace-head is currently on display in the Royal Pump Room Museum in Harrogate.[850]

Figure A.12

Figure A.13 Conical mace-head, described in the museum records as being composed of black syenite with white marbling.[851] The mace-head is described as Predynastic and has been dated to c. 3200 B.C.E.; it is 19.98 mm in height, 74.56 mm in width (at the widest point) and weighs 120 g.[852] The mace-head has a well drilled central piercing and is in excellent condition: "there is little or no damage to the mace-head, not even around the edges, which are the most susceptible to wear and tear".[853] This mace-head is currently on display in the Royal Pump Room Museum.[854]

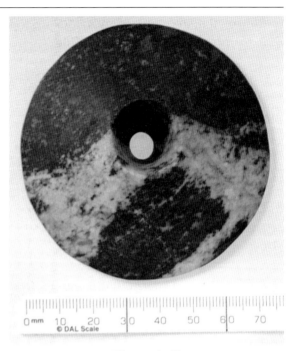

Figure A.14 Conical stone mace-head composed of black syenite with

Figure A.13

white marbling, tentatively dated to the Predynastic period c. 3200 B.C.E.[855] There is no recorded provenance for this mace-head, which is 29.14 mm in height, 75.34

mm in width (at the widest point) and a weight of 140 g.[856] It is in relatively good condition with little damage apparent on either the edges or the main body of the mace-head, though there are a couple of small chips visible on the underside. This mace-head is currently displayed in the Royal Pump Room Museum.[857]

Figure A.14

Figure A.15 Conical stone mace-head described in the museum records as being a "green-specked hard white stone".[858] There is no record on the "exact nature and identification of the stone used, though it is possibly a form of syenite (syenodiortite)".[859] The mace-head has been dated to the Predynastic period, c. 3200 B.C.E., and clearly has the word 'Abydos'

written on it in ink, suggesting a find-site of Abydos.[860] This mace-head was the only one in the Harrogate Museum Collection to have a 'Field Collection' date: 1800 C.E.[861] The mace-head is 30.52 mm in height, 70.62 mm in width (at the widest point) and a weight of 100 g, and there is a drilled central piercing with some moderate damage and chipping to the edges, which show the darker colours underneath the white of the stone more clearly.[862] This mace-head is currently on display in the Royal Pump Room Museum.[863]

Figure A.16

Figure A.16 Conical stone mace-head with a well drilled, smoothed central piercing, stated as being Predynastic and having been discovered at the site of Abydos.[864] It is described as being composed of a hard white stone, with green speckles.[865] However, there has been some confusion with the records as "the mace-head appears to be composed of a dark material, of almost dark green and black colouring, with some patches of red colouring. It would appear to be some form of igneous stone, and the material used for this mace-head resembles some examples of syenite".[866] The mace-head is 17.03 mm in height, 54.79 mm in width (at the widest point) and has a weight of 50 g; there is significant wear around the edges of the mace-head and many scratches on the main body.[867] I do believe that, while this could be either depositional or post-depositional (excavation and display) damage, it could be a result of its use in combat.[868]

Figure A.17

Figure A.17 Piriform (or globular) mace-head of yellow limestone which is Predynastic or Early Dynastic in type. There is no specific date or location recorded since the mace-head is marked incorrectly with the number 3675.[869] The mace-head is 52.15 mm in height, 56.60 mm in width (at the widest point) and weighs 240 g, and has a large central piercing which was probably drilled using a bow drill.[870] Although the mace-head is in good condition, there is some evidence of damage, "with a large indentation or chip in the side being the most noticeable which, as with the other mace-heads, could be due to use in combat, depositional damage or excavation damage".[871]

Bibliography

Adams, B. (1988) *Egyptian Mummies*. Princes Risborough: Shire Publications Ltd.

Aldred, C. (1988a) *The Egyptians*. London: Thames and Hudson Ltd.

Aldred, C. (1988b) 'The Foreign Gifts Offered to Pharaoh', *The Journal of Egyptian Archaeology* 56, 105-116.

Alexander, R. McN. and Bennet-Clark, H. C. (1977) 'Storage of elastic strain energy in muscle and other tissues', *Nature*, 265, 114-17.

anon (2003) 'Digital Egypt/Amarna: UC 376a'

http://www.digitalegypt.ucl.ac.uk/amarna/uc376a.html. Page consulted 11 March 2013.

Arnold, D. (1996) *The royal women of Amarna: images of beauty from ancient Egypt*. New York: Metropolitan Museum of Art.

Baines, J. and Eyre, C. J. (1983) 'Four notes on literacy', *Gottinger Miszellen* 6, 65-96.

Baines, J. and Malek, J. (2000) *Cultural Atlas of Ancient Egypt*. New York: Checkmark Books.

Baumgartel, E. J. (1970) *Petrie's Naqada Excavation: A Supplement*. London: Bernard Quaritch.

Blackman, A. M. (1921) 'On the Position of Women in the Ancient Egyptian Hierarchy', *The Journal of Egyptian Archaeology* 7 (1/2), 8-30.

Boutell, C. (1893) *Arms and Armour*. London: Reeves & Turner.

Breasted, J. H. (1906) *Ancient Records of Egypt, III*. New York: Russell & Russell, re-issue 1962.

Breasted, J. H. (2015) *The battle of Kadesh: a study in the earliest known military strategy – Scholar's Choice Edition*. Scholar's Choice, New York.

Bryan, B. M. (1984) 'Evidence for Female Literacy from Theban Tombs of the New Kingdom', *Bulletin of the Egyptological Seminar* 6, 17-32.

Bull, L. (1942) 'An Egyptian Funerary Model of a Helmet', *The Metropolitan Museum of Art Bulletin* 37 (2), 41-42.

Burridge, N. nd 'Bronze Age Swords/Egyptian and Near East' http://www.bronze-age-swords.com/Egyptian_and%20_Near_East.htm. Page consulted 20 January 2012.

Callender, G. (1988) 'A Critical Examination of the Reign of Hatshepsut', *Ancient History* 18 (2), 86-102.

Callender, V. G. (1992) 'Female Officials in Ancient Egypt and Egyptian Historians' in B. Garlick, S. Dixon, and P. Allen (eds) *Stereotypes of Women in Power: Historical Perspectives and Revisionist Views* 11-35. New York: Greenwood Press.

Carter, H. (2004) *The Tomb of Tutankhamun. Volume 3: The annexe and treasury.* London: Duckworth.

Černy, J. (1973) *Community of Workmen at Thebes in the Ramesside Period.* Cairo: Institut Français d'Archéologie Orientale.

Clayton, P. A. (1995) *Chronicle of the Pharaohs: The Reign-by-Reign Record of the Rulers and Dynasties of Ancient Egypt.* London: Thames and Hudson Ltd.

Cline, W. (1948) 'Notes on Cultural Innovations in Dynastic Egypt', *Southwestern Journal of Anthropology* 4 (1), 1-30.

Cook, R. M. (1937) 'Amasis and the Greeks in Egypt', *The Journal of Hellenic Studies* 57 (2), 227-237.

Cotterel, A. (2004) *Chariot: The Astounding Rise and Fall of the World's First War Machine.* London: Pimlico.

Cottrell, L. (1968) *Warrior Pharaohs.* London: Evans Bros.

Curto, S. (1971) *The Military Art of the Ancient Egyptians [Pamphlet No. 3 of the Egyptian Museum of Turin].* Turin: Pozzo Gros Monti S.p.A.

Dahl, J. nd 'Ancient Egypt Map' https://commons.wikimedia.org/wiki/File:Ancient_Egypt_map-en.svg. Page consulted 24 January 2016.

Darnell, J. C. (2003) 'The Rock Inscriptions of Tjehemau at Abisko', *Zeitschrift für* Ägyptische *Sprache und Altertumskunde* 130, 33-34.

Darnell, J. C., and Manassa, C. (2007) *Tutankhamun's Armies: Battle and Conquest during Ancient Egypt's Late Eighteenth Dynasty.* Hoboken: John Wiley & Sons.

Darnell, J. et al. (2005) 'Two Early Alphabetic Inscriptions from the Wadi el-Ḥôl: New Evidence for the Origin of the Alphabet from the Western Desert of Egypt', *The Annual of the American Schools of Oriental Research* 59, 63-124.

Davies, V. W. (1987) *Catalogue of Ancient Antiquities in the British Museum. VIII. Tools and Weapons I. Axes*. London: British Museum Publications.

Davies, W. (1992) *Masking the Blow*. Oxford: University of California Press.

Dawson, W. R. (1925) 'A Bronze Dagger of the Hyksos Period', *The Journal of Egyptian Archaeology* 11 (3/4), 216-217.

De Buck, A. (1970) *Egyptian Readingbook*. Leiden: Nederlandsch Archaeologisch-Philologiscal Instituut Voor Het Nabije Oosten.

de Garis Davies, N. (1906) *Rock Tombs of El-Amarna, part 4: Tombs of Penthu, Manhu, and others*. London: Egypt Exploration Fund.

De Souza, P. (ed) (2008) *The Ancient World at War*. London: Thames and Hudson Ltd.

Dean, R. A. (2009) 'The mace in Pharaonic Egypt: a multidisciplinary study incorporating a literary review, a catalogue of unpublished material, and the results of experimental archaeology', unpublished MA dissertation, University of York.

Dean, R. A. (2013) *'Women, weaponry and warfare: A multidisciplinary study of the use of weapons by women in Dynastic Egypt', unpublished M.Phil dissertation, University of York.*

Dunn, J. (2011) 'Amenhotep III, the Ninth King of Egypt's Eighteenth Dynasty' http://www.touregypt.net/featurestories/amenhotep3.htm. Page consulted 17 September 2011.

Dunn, J. (nd) 'The Amarna Period of King Akhenaten in Egypt/The Amarna Period' http://www.touregypt.net/featurestories/amarnaperiod.htm. Page consulted 20 June 2014.

Edwards, I. E. S. (1960) 'Two Egyptian Sculptures in Relief', *The British Museum Quarterly* 23 (1), 9-11.

Ellacott, S. E. (1962) *Armour and Blade*. London: Abelard-Schuman.

Erfan, M. *et al.* (2009) 'Cranial Trauma in Ancient Egyptians from the Bahriyah Oasis, Greco-Roman Period', *Research Journal of Medicine and Medical Sciences* 4 (1), 78-84.

Erman, A. (1978) *The Ancient Egyptians, A Sourcebook of their Writings, transl. By A. M. Blackman, with Introduction by W. K. Simpson*. New York: Peter Smith Publishers Inc.

Ertman, E. L. (1976) 'The Cap-Crown of Nefertiti: Its Function and Probable Origin', *Journal of the American Research Center in Egypt* 13, 63-67.

Faulkner, R. O. (1953) 'Egyptian Military Organization', *The Journal of Egyptian Archaeology* 39, 32-47.

Filer, J. M. (1992) 'Head Injuries in Egypt and Nubia: A Comparison of Skulls from Giza and Kerma', *The Journal of Egyptian Archaeology* 78, 281-285.

Fischer, H. G. (1961) 'The Nubian Mercenaries of Gebelein during the First Intermediate Period', *Kush* 9, 44-80.

Fletcher, J. (2004) *The Search for Nefertiti*. London: Hodder.

Fletcher, J. (2007) *The Harrogate Ancient Egyptian Collection* (unpublished catalogue).

Galloway, A. (ed) (1999) *Broken bones: anthropological analysis of blunt force trauma*. Springfield: Charles C. Thomas.

Galloway, A. *et al.* (1999) 'The Role of Forensic Anthropology in Trauma analysis', in A. Galloway (ed) *Broken bones: anthropological analysis of blunt force trauma*. Springfield: Charles C. Thomas.

Gardiner, A. H. (1941) 'Tut 'ankhamun's Gold Dagger', *The Journal of Egyptian Archaeology* 27, 1.

Gardiner, A. H. (1954) 'The Tomb of Queen Twosre', *The Journal of Egyptian Archaeology* 40, 40-44.

Gardiner, A. H. (1955) 'A Unique Funerary Liturgy', *The Journal of Egyptian Archaeology* 41, 9-17.

Gaunt, C. L. (2011) 'The research potential and significance of the Egyptian collections within Yorkshire museums', unpublished MA thesis, University of York.

Gnirs, A. M. (1999) 'Ancient Egypt' in K. Raaflaub and N. Rosenstein (eds) *War and Society in the Ancient and Medieval Worlds: Asia, the Mediterranean, Europe, and Mesoamerica* 71-104. London: Harvard University Press.

Graves-Brown, C. (2010) *Dancing for Hathor: Women in Ancient Egypt*. London: Bloomsbury Continuum.

Groenewegen-Frankfort, H. A., and Ashmole, B. (1967) *The Ancient World*. New York: New American Library.

Habachi, L. (1957) 'Two Graffiti at Sehēl from the Reign of Queen Hatshepsut', *Journal of Near Eastern Studies* 16 (2), 88-104.

Hayes, W. C. (1953) *The Sceptre of Egypt: Part I*. New York: Metropolitan Museum of Art.

Hayes, W. C. (1978) *The Scepter of Egypt: Part I*. New York: Metropolitan Museum of Art.

Hayes, W. C. (1990) *The Scepter of Egypt, Part II*. New York: The Metropolitan Museum of Art.

Healy, M. (1993), *Qadesh, 1300BC: Clash of Warriors*. Osprey Publishing, Oxford.

Hoffmeier, J. K. (1983) 'Some Egyptian Motifs Related to Warfare and Enemies and Their Old Testament Counterparts', *The Ancient World* 6 (1-4), 53-70.

Hulit, T. and Richardson, T. (2007) 'The warriors of Pharaoh: experiments with new Kingdom scale armour, archery and chariots' in B. Molloy (ed) *The Cutting Edge: Studies in Ancient and Medieval Combat* 52-63. Stroud: Tempus Publishing Limited.

Jánosi, P. (1992) 'The Queens Ahhotep I and Ahhotep II and Egypt's Foreign Relations', *Journal of Ancient Chronology* 5, 99-105.

Kanawati, N. (2001) 'A Female Guard Buried In The Teti Cemetery', *The Australian Centre for Egyptology* 12, 65-70.

Lange, K. and Hirmer, M. (1957) *Egypt: architecture, sculpture, painting in three thousand years*. London: Phaidon Press.

Lesko, B. (1996) *The Remarkable Women of Ancient Egypt*. Providence: B. C. Scribe Publications.

Lichtheim, M. (1976) *Ancient Egyptian Literature: A Book of Readings*. Vol. 2, *The New Kingdom*. Berkeley: University of California Press.

Mace, A. C. and Winlock, H. E. (1916a) 'The Tomb of Senebtisi', *The Journal of Egyptian Archaeology* 11 (12), 257-259.

Mace, A. C. and Winlock, H. E. (1916b) *The Tomb of Senebtisi at Lisht*. New York: Metropolitan Museum of Art.

Malek, J. (1997) 'The locusts on the daggers of Ahmose', in E. Goring *et al* (eds) *Chief of seers. Egyptian studies in memory of Cyril Aldred* 207-219. London and New York: Kegan Paul International.

Mallory-Greenough, L. M. (2002) 'The Geographical, Spatial, and Temporal Distribution of Predynastic and First Dynasty Basalt Vessels', *The Journal of Egyptian Archaeology* 88, 67-93.

Maspero, G. (1886) 'Procès Verbal de L'ouverture des Momies de Seti i et Seqenenra Taâaqen', *American Journal of Archaeology and History of Fine Arts* 2 (3), 331-333.

Maspero, G. (ed. A. H. Sayce, trans. M. L. McClure) (1918) History of Egypt, Chaldaea, Syria, Babylonia, and Assyria, Volume 4 (of 12). EBook: Project Gutenberg (www.gutenberg.org/ebooks/17324).

Mays, S. (2010) *The Archaeology of Human Bones*. London: Routledge.

McDermott, B. (2004) *Warfare in Ancient Egypt*. Stroud: Sutton Publishing Limited.

McEwen, E. (1979) 'The chahar-kham or 'four-curved' bow of India' in R. Elgood (ed) *Islamic Arms and Armour* 89-96. London: Scolar.

McLeod, W. (1970) *Composite Bows from the Tomb of Tut'ankhaman.* Oxford: Griffith

Meskell, L. M. (2004) *Archaeologies of Social Life.* Oxford: Blackwell.

Miller, R., McEwen, E. and Bergman, C. (1986) 'Experimental Approaches to Ancient near Eastern Archery', *World Archaeology* 18 (2), 178-195.

Millet, N. B. (1990) 'The Narmer Macehead and Related Objects' *Journal of the American Research Center in Egypt* 27, 53-59.

Molloy, B. (ed) (2007) *The Cutting Edge: Studies in Ancient and Medieval Combat.* Stroud: Tempus Publishing Limited.

Moran, W. (1992) *The Amarna Letters.* Baltimore: Johns Hopkins University Press.

Murnane, W. J. (1997) 'Three Kingdoms and Thirty-Four Dynasties' in D. P. Silverman (ed) *Ancient Egypt* 148-165. London: Duncan Baird.

Needler, W. (1962) 'A Dagger of Ahmose I', *Archaeology* 15 (3), 172-175.

Newman, R. and Serpico, M. (2000) 'Adhesives and binders' in P T Nicholson and I Shaw (eds), *Ancient Egyptian Materials and Technology*, 475-494. Cambridge: University Press.

Pahor, A. L. and Cole, J. (1995) 'The Birmingham mummy: the first torticollis in history', *The Journal of Laryngology & Otology* 109, 273-276.

Parsche, F., Betz, P. and Nerlich, N. G. (1996) 'Possible Evidence for Homicide in an Egyptian Mummy Head', *International Journal of Osteoarchaeology* 6, 326-332.

Peck, W. H., and Ross, J. G. (1978) *Egyptian Drawings.* London: Thames & Hudson.

Petrie, W. M. F. (1898) *Deshahsheh.* London: The Egypt Exploration Society.

Petrie, W. M. F. and Quibell, J. E. (1896) *Naqada and Ballas.* London: Bernard Quaritch.

Price, F. G. H. (1885) 'Notes Upon Some Ancient Egyptian Implements', *The Journal of the Anthropological Institute of Great Britain and Ireland* 14, 56-64.

Rainey, A. F. (1965) 'The Military Personnel of Ugarit', *Journal of Near Eastern Studies* 24 (1/2), 17-27.

Redford, D. B. (1967) *History and Chronology of the Eighteenth Dynasty.* Toronto: University of Toronto Press.

Redford, D. B. (1997) 'Egypt and the World Beyond' in D. P. Silverman (ed) *Ancient Egypt* 40-57. London: Duncan Baird.

Reeves, N. (1990) *The Complete Tutankhamun.* London: Thames & Hudson.

Reeves, C. N. (1992) *The Complete Tutankhamun: The King, The Tomb, The Royal Treasure.* London: Thames and Hudson Ltd.

Richardson, H. C. (1934) 'Iron, Prehistoric and Ancient', *American Journal of Archaeology* 38 (4), 555-583.

Robins, G. (2004) *Women in Ancient Egypt.* London: The British Museum Press.

Roehrig, C. H., Dreyfus, R., and Keller, C. A. (2005) *Hatshepsut: from queen to pharaoh.* New York: Metropolitan Museum of Art.

Samson, J. (2002) *Nefertiti and Cleopatra: Queen-Monarchs of Ancient Egypt.* New York: Barnes & Noble Books.

Säve-Söderbergh, T. (1951) 'The Hyksos Rule in Egypt', *The Journal of Egyptian Archaeology* 37, 53-71.

Sayce, A. H. (1903) 'The Hyksos in Egypt', *The Biblical World* 21 (5), 347-355.

Schneider, T. (2003) *Ausländer in Ägypten während des Mittleren Reiches und der Hyksoszeit, Volume 2, Die ausländische Bevölkerung.* Wiesbaden: Otto Harrassowitz.

Schulman, A. R. (1964) 'Some Observations on the Military Background of the Amarna Period', *Journal of the American Research Center in Egypt* 3, 51-69.

Shaw, G. J. (2009) 'The Death of King Seqenenre Tao', *Journal of the American Research Center in Egypt* 45, 159-176.

Shaw, I. (1991) *Egyptian Warfare and Weapons.* Princes Risborough: Shire Publications Ltd.

Shaw, I. (1997) 'The Settled World' in D. P. Silverman (ed) *Ancient Egypt* 68-79. London: Duncan Baird.

Shaw, I. and Boatright, D. (2008) 'Ancient Egyptian Warfare' in P. De Souza (ed) *The Ancient World at War,* 29-46. London: Thames and Hudson Ltd.

Shaw, I. and Nicholson, P. (1997) *The British Museum Dictionary of Ancient Egypt.* London: British Museum Press.

Silverman, D. P. (ed) (1997) *Ancient Egypt.* London: Duncan Baird.

Smith, G. Elliot (2000) *The Royal Mummies.* London: Duckworth. (Facsimile reprint of 1912 edition).

Smither, P. C. (1945) 'The Semnah Despatches', *The Journal of Egyptian Archaeology* 31, 3-10.

Spalinger, A. J. (2005) *War in Ancient Egypt.* Oxford: Blackwell Publishing Ltd.

Spradley, M. K. *et al.* (2011) 'Spatial patterning of vulture scavenged human remains', *Forensic Science International* (doi:10.1016/j. forsciint.2011.11.030).

Steindorff, G., and Seele, K. (1957) *When Egypt Ruled the East*. Chicago: University of Chicago Press.

Stevenson Smith, W. (1942) 'Recent Discoveries in the Egyptian Department', *Bulletin of the Museum of Fine Arts* 40 (239), 42-49.

Stonborough, W. (2011) 'The Shields of Pharaoh: a study of ancient Egyptian protective military equipment, incorporating an analysis of skin-based materials, a review of current knowledge, and the results of experimental archaeology', unpublished MA dissertation, University of York.

Tangri, D. (1992) 'A reassessment of the origins of the predynastic in Upper Egypt', *Proceedings of the Prehistoric Society* 58, 112-125.

Teeter, E. (1997) 'The Life of Ritual' in D. P. Silverman (ed) *Ancient Egypt* 148-165. London: Duncan Baird.

ten Berge, R. L. and van de Goot, F. R. W (2002) 'Seqenenre Taa II, the violent death of a pharaoh', *Journal of Clinical Pathology* 55, 232.

Tirard, H. M. (1915) 'The Soldiers of Ancient Egypt', *The Journal of Egyptian Archaeology* 2 (4), 229-233.

Troy, L. (1986) *Patterns of Queenship in ancient Egyptian myth and history.* Uppsala: Acta Universitatis Upsaliensis.

Vogelsang-Eastwood, G. M. (1999) *Tutankhamun's Wardrobe*. Rotterdam: Barjesteh van Waalvijk van Doorn.

Wainwright, G. A. (1932) 'Iron in Egypt', *The Journal of Egyptian Archaeology* 18 (1/2), 3-15.

Ward, W. A. (1961) 'Comparative Studies in Egyptian and Ugaritic', *Journal of Near Eastern Studies* 20 (1), 31-40.

Wengrow, D. (2006) *The Archaeology of Early Egypt: Social Transformations in North-East Africa, 10,000 to 2650 BC*. Cambridge: Cambridge University Press.

Western, A. C. and McLeod, W. (1995) 'Woods Used In Egyptian Bows and Arrows', *The Journal of Egyptian Archaeology* 81, 77-94.

White, T. D. and Folkens, P. A. (2005) *The Human Bone Manual*. Oxford: Elsevier Academic.

Wilkinson, T. A. H. (1999) *Early Dynastic Egypt*. London: Routledge.

Wilkinson, T. A. H. (2000) 'What a King Is This: Narmer and the Concept of the Ruler' *The Journal of Egyptian Archaeology* 86, 23-32.

Wilkinson, T. A. H (2010) *The Rise and Fall of Ancient Egypt: The History of a Civilisation from 3000 BC to Cleopatra*. London: Bloomsbury.

Wilson, H. (1997) *People of the Pharaohs: From Peasant to Courtier*. London: Michael O'Mara Books Limited.

Wilson, J. A. (1951) *The Culture of Ancient Egypt*. Chicago: University of Chicago Press.

Winlock, H. E. (1924) 'The Tombs of the Kings of the Seventeenth Dynasty at Thebes', *The Journal of Egyptian Archaeology* 10 (3/4), 217-277.

Winlock, H. E. (2007) *The Slain Soldiers of Neb-Hepet-Re Mentu-Hotpe*. Mansfield Centre: Martino Publishing.

Wrobel, G. D. (2004) 'The benefits of an archaeology of gender for Predynastic Egypt', in K. A. Pyburn (ed) *Ungendering Civilization* 156-178. London: Routledge.

Yon, M. (2000) 'Daily Life', *Near Eastern Archaeology* 63 (4), 200-201.

Zorn, J. (1991) 'LÚ. pa-ma-ḫa-a in EA 162:74 and the Role of the MHR in Egypt and Ugarit', *Journal of Near Eastern Studies* 50 (2), 129-138.

Other works to read:

Aldred, C. (1992) *Egypt to the end of the Old Kingdom*. London: Thames and Hudson Ltd.

Hall, H. R. (1926) 'Egyptian Antiquities', *The British Museum Quarterly* 1 (2), 42-43.

Harrison, P. (2004) *Great Battles of the Ancient World*. London: Virgin Books.

Holmes, R. (2006) *Weapons: A Visual History of Arms and Armour*. London: Dorling Kindersley.

Needler, W. (1984) *Predynastic and Archaic Egypt in the Brooklyn Museum*. Brooklyn NY: The Brooklyn Museum.

Petrie, W. M. F., Wainwright, G. A., and Gardiner, A. H. (1913) *Tarkham I and Memphis V*. London: School of Archaeology in Egypt.

Quibell, J. E. (2006) *Hierakonpolis: Part 1 (Unabridged Facsimile)*. London: Elibron Classics.

Taylor, J. H. (2001) *Death and the Afterlife in Ancient Egypt*. London: The British Museum Press.

Wallis Budge, E. A. (1997) *The Egyptian Heaven and Hell (Unabridged Facsimile)*. Chicago: Open Court.

Index

Endnotes

(Listed by Chapter)

Warfare in Ancient Egypt

1   See Mark Healy 1993, *Qadesh, 1300BC: Clash of Warriors.* Osprey Publishing, Oxford; James Henry Breasted 2015, *The battle of Kadesh: a study in the earliest known military strategy – Scholar's Choice Edition.* Scholar's Choice, New York.
2   Curto 1971, 3.
3   Redford 1997, 51.
4   Hoffmeier 1983, 53.
5   Ibid, 53.
6   Ibid, 53; Curto 1971, 3.
7   Hoffmeier 1983, 54; Dean 2009.
8   Groenewegen-Frankfort and Ashmole 1967, 24; Hoffmeier 1983, 54.
9   Hoffmeier 1983, 54; Shaw 1991, 9.
10 De Buck 1970, 56.11; cited in Hoffmeier 1983, 54.
11 Baines and Eyre 1983.
12 Hoffmeier 1983, 56; 59.
13 Ibid, 69; De Buck 1970, 49.4.
14 Hoffmeier 1983, 60.
15 Curto 1971, 3-4.
16 Shaw 1991, 25.
17 Ibid, 25.
18 Ibid, 25; Wilson 1997, 166.
19 Wilson 1997, 166.
20 Ibid, 169.
21 Ibid, 169.
22 Shaw 1991, 25.
23 Ibid, 25.
24 Wilson 1997, 166.
25 Ibid, 168.
26 Shaw 1991, 25.
27 Ibid, 25.
28 Wilson 1997, 168.
29 Shaw 1991, 25.
30 Ibid, 25.
31 Ibid, 25.
32 Ibid, 25.
33 Ibid, 26; Smither 1945; Gardiner 1955.
34 Shaw 1991, 26.

35   Darnell and Manassa 2007, 62-63.
36   Ibid, 63.
37   Ibid, 63.
38   Shaw 1991, 26.
39   Ibid, 26-27.
40   Redford 1997, 51.
41   Ibid, 51.
42   Ibid, 51.
43   Darnell 2003; Darnell and Manassa 2007, 63.
44   Darnell and Manassa 2007, 63.
45   Shaw 1991, 29.
46   Ibid, 29.
47   Ibid, 29.
48   de Garis Davies 1906, pls. 17 and 19; Darnell and Manassa 2007, 63.
49   Shaw 1991, 30.
50   Ibid, 30.
51   Wilson 1997, 185.
52   Shaw 1991, 27.
53   Ibid, 27-28.
54   Ibid, 28.
55   Darnell and Manassa 2007, 61.
56   Ibid, 61.
57   Redford 1997, 51.
58   Ibid, 51; Darnell and Manassa 2007, 61.
59   Darnell and Manassa 2007, 61.
60   Ibid, 62; Shaw 1991, 27-28.
61   Darnell and Manassa 2007, 62.
62   Schulman 1964; Darnell and Manassa 2007, 62.
63   Redford 1997, 51.
64   Ibid, 51.
65   Ibid, 51.
66   Shaw and Nicholson 1997, 64.
67   Shaw 1991, 41.
68   Rainey 1965, 58.
69   Aldred 1988b, 154.
70   Darnell and Manassa 2007, 64.
71   Ibid, 64.
72   Ibid, 63.
73   Ibid, 63.
74   Ibid, 64.
75   Zorn 1991, 136.
76   Aldred 1988b, 154.
77   Darnell and Manassa 2007, 64.
78   Ibid, 64.
79   Ibid, 67.
80   Ibid, 67.
81   Darnell and Manassa 2007, 67.

82   Fischer 1961; Darnell and Manassa 2007, 67.
83   Schneider 2003, 92-93; Darnell and Manassa 2007, 67; Shaw 1991, 30; Wilson 1997, 176.
84   Černy 1973; Darnell and Manassa 2007, 67; Wilson 1997, 176.
85   Moran 1992, 139 and 169; Darnell and Manassa 2007, 67.
86   Darnell and Manassa 2007, 68.
87   Darnell *et al.* 2005, 87; Darnell and Manassa 2007, 68.
88   Shaw 1991, 60; Wilson 1997, 184.
89   Shaw 1991, 60.
90   Ibid, 60.
91   Spalinger 2005, 18-19; Wilson 1997, 184.
92   Spalinger 2005, 3,46, 53.
93   Shaw 1991, 62; Spalinger 2005, 254.
94   Shaw 1991, 62.
95   Spalinger 2005, 254.
96   Shaw 1991, 62; Spalinger 2005, 55.
97   Spalinger 2005, 255.
98   Ibid, 254-255.
99   Shaw 1991, 62.
100   Ibid, 62-63.
101   Ibid, 63.
102   Shaw 1991, 63; Spalinger 2005, 255.
103   Spalinger 2005, 56.
104   Ibid, 56.

2. Weapons in Ancient Egypt

105   Shaw and Nicholson 1997, 32.
106   Shaw 1991, 43; Shaw & Boatright 2008, 40; Stonborough 2011, 61.
107   McDermott 2004, 34.
108   Shaw and Nicholson 1997, 71.
109   McDermott 2004, 34.
110   Ibid, 34.
111   Wengrow 2006, 249.
112   Davies 1987.
113   Ibid, 27.
114   Ibid, 27.
115   Davies 1987.
116   Ibid, 31.
117   Ibid, 33.
118   Ibid, 36.
119   Ibid, 38.
120   McDermott 2004, 72.
121   Ibid, 72.
122   Ibid, 74.
123   Ibid, 76.
124   Ibid, 74.
125   Ibid, 74; Davies 1987, 23.
126   McDermott 2004, 74; Shaw and Boatright 2008, 40.

127 Spalinger 2005, 16.
128 Davies 1987.
129 McDermott 2004, 74.
130 Ibid, 74; Davies 1987.
131 Shaw and Boatright 2008, 40.
132 McDermott 200, 74-76.
133 Shaw and Boatright 2008, 40; Spalinger 2005, 16.
134 McDermott 2004, 77.
135 Shaw and Nicholson 1997, 255; McDermott 2004, 77.
136 Davies 1987.
137 Shaw and Nicholson 1997, 219.
138 McDermott 2004, 162.
139 Ibid, 162.
140 Ibid, 162.
141 Ibid, 162.
142 Shaw and Boatright 2008, 40.
143 McDermott 2004, 162.
144 Ibid, 162.
145 Ibid, 162.
146 Shaw and Boatright 2008, 40.
147 McDermott 2004, 164.
148 Davies 1987, 45.
149 Ibid, 45.
150 Ibid, 45.
151 Ibid, 40-41.
152 Ibid, 40.
153 McDermott 2004, 164; Shaw and Boatright 2008, 39.
154 McDermott 2004, 164.
155 Shaw and Boatright 2008, 39; Price 1885, 58.
156 Davies 1987, 46.
157 Ibid, 46.
158 Ibid, 46.
159 McDermott 2004, 162.
160 Ibid, 76.
161 Spalinger 2005, 120.
162 Ibid, 123.
163 Ibid, 123.
164 McDermott 2004, 163-164.
165 Ibid, 164.
166 Shaw and Boatright 2008, 40.
167 McDermott 2004, 31.
168 Ibid, 31.
169 Shaw and Boatright 2008, 40.
170 Ibid, 40.
171 McDermott 2004, 31.
172 Ibid, 31.
173 Shaw and Boatright 2008, 40.

174 Ibid, 43.
175 Ibid; Shaw 1991, 42.
176 Western and McLeod 1995, 77.
177 Ibid, 79-80.
178 Ibid, 79.
179 Ibid, 80.
180 Ibid, 80.
181 Ibid, 80.
182 Ibid, 80.
183 Ibid, 77.
184 Spalinger 2005, 6.
185 Ibid, 17.
186 Miller *et al.* 1986.
187 Ibid, 178.
188 Ibid, 178.
189 Miller *et al.* 1986, 183; Alexander and Bennet-Clark 1977.
190 Miller *et al.* 1986, 183; McEwen 1979, 91.
191 Miller *et al.* 1986, 183; McLeod 1970.
192 Shaw and Boatright 2008, 43.
193 Ibid, 43.
194 McDermott 2004, 129; Curto 1971, 11; Aldred 1988a, 142-143; Shaw and Boatright 2008, 40;
Säve-Söderbergh 1951, 61.
195 Shaw and Boatright 2008, 43.
196 McDermott 2004, 67.
197 Shaw and Boatright 2008, 43.
198 Wengrow 2006, 47; Tangri 1992.
199 Wengrow 2006, 47.
200 Winlock 2007, 23-24.
201 Ibid, 11-14.
202 McDermott 2004, 67.
203 Shaw and Boatright 2008, 43.
204 Ibid, 43.
205 T. O'Connor, pers. comm. March 2013.
206 Spalinger 2005, 196.
207 Ibid, 121.
208 Shaw and Boatright 2008, 38.
209 Spalinger 2005, 8.
210 Darnell and Manassa 2007, 77.
211 McDermott 2004, 88; Aldred 1988a, 142; Säve-Söderbergh 1951, 61.
212 McDermott 2004, 129.
213 Curto 1971, 11.
214 McDermott 2004, 101.
215 Aldred 1988a, 142.
216 Ibid, 143.
217 Spalinger 2005, 15.
218 Ibid, 12.

219 Shaw and Boatright 2008, 38.
220 Aldred 1988a, 190.
221 Ibid, 190.
222 Erman 1978, 194-197; Aldred 1988a, 192.
223 Aldred 1988a, 190.
224 anon (2003).
225 Spalinger 2005, 178.
226 McDermott 2004, 129.
227 Curto 1971, 18.
228 Redford 2003, 51.
229 McDermott 2004, 131.
230 Ibid, 101.
231 Ibid, 101.
232 Ibid, 130.
233 Shaw and Boatright 2008, 38.
234 Ibid, 38; Cotterell 2004, 92.
235 Cotterell 2004, 92.
236 Shaw and Boatright 2008, 38.
237 Ibid, 38.
238 Ibid, 38.
239 Shaw 1991, 41.
240 McDermott 2004, 129.
241 Shaw and Boatright 2008, 38.
242 Spalinger 2005, 18.
243 Ibid, 194.
244 Ibid, 194.
245 Ibid, 196.
246 Gnirs 1999, 84; Lichtheim 1976, 41-42.
247 Gnirs 1999, 87.
248 Wengrow 2006, 52-53.
249 Shaw and Nicholson 1997, 167.
250 McDermott 2004, 37.
251 Ibid, 35.
252 Dean 2009, 38.
253 Ibid, 38.
254 Shaw 1991, 31.
255 Dean 2009.
256 Ibid, 38.
257 Ibid.
258 Davies 1992, 203; Dean 2009, 9.
259 Aldred 1988a, 70; Dean 2009, 9.
260 Aldred 1988a, 70; Dean 2009, 9.
261 Davies 1992, 224; Dean 2009, 9.
262 Wilkinson 2000, 25; Dean 2009, 9.
263 Aldred 1988a, 79; Dean 2009, 9.
264 Millet 1990, 55.
265 Ibid, 55.

266 Ibid, 56; Dean 2009, 10.
267 Millet 1990, 56; Dean 2009, 10.
268 Shaw and Nicholson 1997, 197.
269 Davies 1992, 194.
270 Dean 2009, 14.
271 Shaw and Nicholson 1997, 256; Dean 2009, 14.
272 Shaw and Nicholson 1997, 257; Dean 2009, 14.
273 Lange & Hirmer 1957, 311.
274 Shaw and Nicholson 1997, 183.
275 Dean 2009, 15.
276 Ibid, 15.
277 Hayes 1990, 369; Dean 2009, 16.
278 Dean 2009, 16.
279 Shaw and Nicholson 1995, 90; Dean 2009; 17.
280 Dean 2009, 17.
281 Silverman 1997, 107; Teeter 1997, 155; McDermott 2004, 35; Dean 2009, 17.
282 McDermott 2004, 37.
283 Ibid, 36-37.
284 McDermott 2004, 36.
285 Stevenson Smith 1942, 47; Dean 2009, 16.
286 McDermott 2004, 164.
287 Shaw 1991, 37.
288 Hayes 1978, 283.
289 McDermott 2004, 166.
290 Ibid, 166.
291 Säve-Söderbergh 1951, 61.
292 Shaw 1991, 42-43.
293 Darnell and Manassa 2007, 76.
294 Hayes 1990, 68.
295 Ibid, 68.
296 Ibid, 68.
297 McDermott 2004, 164.
298 Richardson 1934, 556.
299 McDermott 2004, 164.
300 Darnell and Manassa 2007, 76.
301 McDermott 2004, 164.
302 Ibid, 166; Hayes 1990, 77.
303 McDermott 2004, 166.
304 Ibid, 167.
305 Hayes 1990, 412.
306 Shaw 1991, 43; Säve-Söderbergh 1951, 61.
307 Hayes 1978, 96.
308 Shaw and Nicholson 1997, 137.
309 Shaw and Boatright 2008, 40.
310 McDermott 2004, 167.
311 Darnell and Manassa 2007, 76.
312 Ibid, 76; Spalinger 2005, 17.

313   Shaw and Boatright 2008, 40.
314   Darnell and Manassa 2007, 76.
315   Carter 2004, 76; Reeves 1992, 177; McDermott 2004, 167.
316   Ibid, 76.
317   Ibid, 137.
318   Ibid, 77; Reeves 1992, 177.
319   Carter 2004, 77; Reeves 1992, 177.
320   Carter 2004, 77; Reeves 1992, 177.
321   Carter 2004, 77.
322   Darnell and Manassa 2007, 76.
323   Carter 2004, 77.
324   Darnell and Manassa 2007, 76.
325   McDermott 2004, 170.
326   Ibid, 170.
327   Spalinger 2005, 194, 198 and 236.
328   McDermott 2004, 167.
329   Ibid, 167.
330   Ibid, 170.
331   Ibid, 170.
332   Ibid, 170.
333   Fletcher 2004, 74.
334   Ibid; 192; 282.
335   Fletcher 2004, 282; Samson 2002, 25.
336   Cline 1948, 4.
337   Price 1885, 58.
338   Shaw and Boatright 2008, 31.
339   Ibid, 31.
340   Shaw 1991, 37.
341   Cline 1948, 16.
342   Shaw and Boatright 2008, 31.
343   Shaw 1991, 43.
344   Mace and Winlock 1916a, 259; Mace and Winlock 1916b, 76-103; 104-105.
345   Hayes 1978, 283; Mace and Winlock 1916b, 104.
346   Hayes 1978, 283.
347   Tirard 1915, 232.
348   Ibid, 232.
349   Sayce 1903, 350; Säve-Söderbergh 1951, 70-71.
350   Sayce 1903, 350; Säve-Söderbergh 1951, 70.
351   Dawson 1925, 216.
352   Ibid, 216.
353   Ibid, 216.
354   Ibid, 216.
355   Shaw and Boatright 2008, 37.
356   Ibid, 37.
357   Jánosi 1992, 104.
358   Ibid, 104.
359   Malek 1997, 207-219.

360 Jánosi 1992, 104.
361 Ibid, 104.
362 Darnell and Manassa 2007, 77.
363 Reeves 1992, 177.
364 Gardiner 1941, 1; Reeves 1992, 177.
365 Gardiner 1941, 1.
366 Ibid, 1; Reeves 1992, 177.
367 Shaw and Boatright 2008, 39; Wainwright 1932, 14.
368 Reeves 1992, 177.
369 Ibid, 177.
370 Ibid, 177.
371 Shaw and Boatright 2008, 39.
372 Wainwright 1932, 14.
373 Reeves 1992, 177; Darnell and Manassa 2007, 77.
374 Shaw and Nicholson 1997.
375 Faulkner 1953, 35.
376 Shaw and Boatright 2008, 29.
377 Ibid, 31-40.
378 Edwards 1960, 9.
379 Ibid, 9.
380 Ibid, 9.
381 Fletcher 2004, 206.
382 Shaw 1991, 31.
383 Ibid, 34; Redford 2003, 51.
384 Shaw 1991, 34.
385 Ibid, 37.
386 Wilson 1997, 169.
387 Shaw 1991, 37.
388 Ibid, 36-37.
389 Ibid, 36-37.
390 Hayes 1978, 166.
391 Ibid, 284.
392 Ibid, 68-69.
393 Ibid, 284-285.
394 Hayes 1990, 215.
395 Ibid, 149.
396 Hayes 1978, 284.
397 Hulit, T. and Richardson, T. (2007) 'The warriors of Pharaoh: experiments with new Kingdom scale armour, archery and chariots'.
398 Spalinger 2005, 172.

Defending Ancient Egypt
399 Shaw 1991, 60.
400 Wilson 1997, 166-167.
401 Ibid, 168.
402 Ibid, 168-169.
403 Shaw 1997, 78, in Silverman (ed) 1997.

404 Ibid, 78.
405 Shaw 1991, 17.
406 Ibid, 17.
407 Shaw 1997, 79, in Silverman (ed) 1997.
408 Shaw 1991, 20.
409 Wilson 1997, 173.
410 Shaw 1997, 79.
411 Ibid, 79.
412 Shaw 1991, 19.
413 Shaw 1997, 78.
414 Ibid, 79.
415 Shaw 1991, 23.
416 Ibid, 23.
417 Boutell 1893, 51-52.
418 Ellacott 1962, 10-11.
419 Wilson 1997, 170; Shaw 1991, 32-34.
420 Shaw 1991, 32-34; Stonborough 2011.
421 Shaw 1991, 32-34.
422 Baines & Malek 2000, 203; Stonborough 2011, 35.
423 Stonborough 2011, 35.
424 Ibid 2011, 35-36.
425 Shaw 1991, 34.
426 McDermott 2004, 53.
427 Ibid, 53.
428 Hayes 1953, 278.
429 Stonborough 2011, 36-37; McDermott 2004, 53; Hayes 1953, 278.
430 Stonborough 2011, 36-37.
431 Ibid, 37.
432 Ibid, 37.
433 Ibid, 37.
434 Shaw 1991, 34.
435 Ibid, 34.
436 Stonborough 2011, 37.
437 Hayes 1953, 278.
438 Stonborough 2011, 38.
439 Ibid, 38.
440 Ibid, 38.
441 Hulit and Richardson 2007, 63.
442 Shaw 1991, 34.
443 Hayes 1953, 278.
444 Ibid, 278.
445 Stonborough 2011, 38.
446 Ibid, 39.
447 Hayes 1953, 278.
448 Stonborough 2011, 39; McDermott 2004, 53; Hayes 1953, 278.
449 Stonborough 2011, 39; Hayes 1953, 278.
450 Stonborough 2011, 39.

451   Ibid; Hayes 1953, 278.
452   Stonborough 2011, 39.
453   Ibid, 39-40.
454   Ibid, 40; Newman and Serpico 2000, 475, 480-492.
455   Stonborough 2011, 40.
456   Ibid.
457   Ibid, 40-41.
458   Ibid, 41.
459   Ibid, 41.
460   Ibid, 41.
461   Ibid, 41; McDermott 2004, 146-148.
462   Stonborough 2011, 41-42.
463   Reeves 1990, 176-177; McDermott 2004, 148.
464   Stonborough 2011, 42; Reeves 1990, 176-177.
465   Ibid, 42.
466   Ibid, 43; Shaw 1991, 43; Hulit and Richardson2007, 53.
467   Bull 1942, 42; Hayes 1953, 278; Shaw 1991, 32; Baines & Malek 2000, 203; McDermott
      2004, 52;
      Stonborough 2011, 22.
468   Hayes 1953, 278; Winlock 2007, 9; Stonborough 2011, 22.
469   Stonborough 2011, 22-23.
470   Winlock 2007, 9.
471   Stonborough 2011, 23.
472   Ibid, 24.
473   Ibid, 24.
474   Ibid, 24.
475   McDermott 2004, 139; Stonborough 2011, 23.
476   Bull 1942, 41-42; Stonborough 2011, 23.
477   Bull 1942, 42, Stonborough 2011, 23.
478   McDermott 2004, 142.
479   Stonborough 2011, 24.
480   Ibid, 24.
481   Shaw 1991, 42.
482   Ibid, 44.
483   Ibid, 32; Baines and Malek 2000, 203.
484   Hayes 1953, 277-278; Stonborough 2011, 25-26.
485   McDermott 2004; Stonborough 2011, 26.
486   Stonborough 2011, 26.
487   Ibid, 26.
488   Ibid, 27.
489   McDermott 2004, 52; Stonborough 2011, 28.
490   Vogelsang-Eastwood 1999, 48; Stonborough 2011, 28.
491   Stonborough 2011, 28.
492   McDermott 2004, 53-54; Stonborough 2011, 28-29.
493   McDermott 2004, 52.
494   Stonborough 2011, 29.
495   Ibid, 29.

496   McDermott 2004, 143; Stonborough 2011, 30.
497   Stonborough 2011, 30.
498   Hulit and Richardson2007, 61; Fletcher 2004, 376-7; Stonborough 2011, 30.
499   Stonborough 2011, 30.
500   Ibid, 30.
501   Ibid, 31.
502   Ibid, 31.
503   Vogelsang-Eastwood 1999, 100-101; Stonborough 2011, 31.
504   Stonborough 2011, 31.
505   Ibid, 32.
506   Hulit and Richardson 2007, 53; Stonborough 2011, 32.
507   Vogelsang-Eastwood 1999, 110; Baines & Malek 2000, 203; Hulit and Richardson2007, 53; Stonborough 2011, 32.
508   Vogelsang-Eastwood 1999, 110; Hulit and Richardson2007, 53; Stonborough 2011, 33.
509   Stonborough 2011, 33.
510   Hayes 1959, 214; 254-5.
511   Hulit and Richardson 2007, 53; Stonborough 2011, 33.
512   Hulit and Richardson 2007, 54-63; Stonborough 2011, 33.
513   Stonborough 2011, 33.
514   Hulit and Richardson 2007, 53, 63; Stonborough 2011, 33.
515   Hulit and Richardson 2007, 54-63.
516   Hulit and Richardson 2007, 54-63; Stonborough 2011, 34.
517   Hulit and Richardson2007, 56, 58-61; Stonborough 2011, 34.
518   Hulit and Richardson 2007, 61; Stonborough 2011, 34.
519   Stonborough 2011, 34.
520   Ibid, 34-35.

Women and Warfare in Ancient Egypt

521   Dean 2009, 42.
522   Petrie and Quibell 1896, 28.
523   Mallory-Greenough 2002, 89.
524   Petrie and Quibell 1896.
525   Mallory-Greenough 2002, 89.
526   Baumgartel 1970, Pl. XLII; Mallory-Greenough 2002, 89.
527   Baumgartel 1970, Pl. XLII.
528   Petrie and Quibell 1896, 28.
529   Ibid, 28.
530   Baumgartel 1970, 6.
531   Callender 1992, 19.
532   Dean 2009, 41.
533   Petrie 1898, 6.
534   Ibid, 6.
535   Ibid, 6.
536   Ibid, 6.
537   Ibid 1898, 6.
538   Dean 2009, 42.
539   Kanawati 2001, 66.

540 Ibid, 66.
541 Ibid, 66.
542 Ibid, 66.
543 Ibid, 67.
544 Ibid, 67.
545 Dean 2009, 43.
546 Hayes 1978, 282-283; Mace and Winlock 1916b, 102-103; 106.
547 Hayes 1978, 282.
548 Ibid, 283; Mace and Winlock 1916b, 102-103; 106.
549 Fletcher 2004, 206.
550 Shaw and Nicholson 1997, 18.
551 Breasted 1906, 29-32.
552 Redford 1967, 69.
553 Jánosi 1992, 99.
554 Lesko 1996, 13; Jánosi 1992, 101.
555 Wilson 1997, 169.
556 Spalinger 2005, 17.
557 Ibid, 17.
558 Lesko 1996, 13.
559 Ibid, 13.
560 Callender 1988, 86.
561 Ibid, 87.
562 Ibid, 87.
563 Ibid, 87.
564 Ibid, 93.
565 Wilson 1951, 175.
566 Ibid, 175.
567 Redford 1967; see also Callender 1988, 93.
568 Cottrell 1968, 73.
569 Ibid, 74.
570 Redford 1967.
571 Habachi 1957, 102; Callender 1988, 93.
572 Callender 1988, 93; e.g. Wilson 1951, 175.
573 Ibid, 93.
574 Ibid, 93.
575 Habachi 1957, 99-100.
576 Callender 1988, 94.
577 Ibid, 94.
578 Stevenson Smith 1942, 47.
579 Ibid, 47.
580 Ibid, 47.
581 Roehrig *et al.* 2005, 202.
582 Fletcher 2004, 214.
583 Ibid.
584 Ibid, 74; 192; 282.
585 Samson 2002, 25.
586 Ibid, 282; Samson 2002, 25; Lesko 1996, 21.

587 Samson 2002, 25.
588 Dean 2009, 15.
589 Samson 2002, 64-65.
590 Ibid, 64-65.
591 Ertman 1976, 63; de Garis Davies 1903, pls X and XVII; Samson 2002, 64-65.
592 Fletcher 2004, 186; Murnane 1997, 35; Lesko 1996, 25; Robins 2004, 50.
593 Lesko 1996, 25.
594 Shaw and Nicholson 1997.
595 Troy 1986, 143.
596 Ibid, 143.
597 Lesko 1996, 25.
598 Gardiner 1954, 40.
599 Ibid, 43.
600 Ibid, 44.
601 Peck 1978, 159; 205.
602 Lesko 1996, 25.
603 Peck 1978, 205.
604 Ibid, 159.
605 Ibid, 159.
606 Ibid, 159.
607 Spalinger 2005, 194.
608 Clayton 1995, 159; Fletcher 2004, 186.
609 Wrobel 2004, 159.
610 Meskell 2004, 85; Dean 2013, 149.
611 Meskell 2004, 97; Dean 2013, 149.
612 Dean 2013, 149.
613 Ibid, 150.
614 Baines and Eyre 1983.

Experimental Archaeology
615 Galloway et al 1999, 25-26.
616 Dean 2009, 36.
617 Ibid, 36.
618 Ibid, 36.
619 Ibid, 36.
620 Dean 2009, 37.
621 Ibid, 36.
622 Ibid, 37.
623 Ibid, 37.
624 Ibid, 38.
625 Dean 2009, 38.
626 Ibid, 38.
627 Dean 2013.
628 Ibid, 38.
629 Dean 2009, 46.
630 Ibid, 36; 39.
631 Ibid, 46.

632 Burridge, nd [a].
633 Davies 1987, 45; Pl. 22.
634 Ibid, 45.
635 Ibid, 44; Pl. 20 and 32.
636 Needler 1962, 173-174.
637 For more information, see Mays 2010.
638 Ibid.
639 Mays 2010, 239.
640 Mays 2010, 238.
641 Galloway 1999, 35.
642 Ibid, 35.
643 Ibid, 23.
644 Ibid, 23.
645 Ibid, 23.
646 Mays 2010, 238.
647 Galloway et al 1999, 23.
648 White & Folkens 2005, 60-62.
649 Mays 2010, 238.
650 Ibid, 244.
651 Carter 2004, 76; 137.
652 Carter 2004, 77; Reeves 1992, 177.
653 Burridge nd [b].
654 T. O'Connor, pers. comm. February 2013.
655 Stonborough 2011, 44.
656 Ibid, 44.
657 Ibid, 44.
658 Dean 2009; Stonborough 2011, 44; Dean 2013.
659 Stonborough 2011, 44-45.
660 Hayes 1953, 278.
661 Stonborough 2011, 45.
662 Ibid, 45.
663 Ibid, 45.
664 Ibid, 45.
665 Ibid, 45.
666 Ibid, 45.
667 Ibid, 46.
668 Ibid, 46.
669 Hayes 1953, 278; Shaw 1991, 34; McDermott 2004, 53.
670 Stonborough 2011, 47.
671 Hayes 1953, 262-274.
672 Stonborough 2011, 48.
673 Ibid, 48.
674 Ibid, 48.
675 Ibid, 48.
676 Ibid, 48.
677 Ibid, 49.
678 Ibid, 49.

679 Ibid, 49.
680 Ibid, 49.
681 Ibid, 50.
682 Ibid, 50.
683 Ibid, 50-51.
684 Ibid, 51.
685 Ibid, 52.
686 Ibid, 52.
687 Ibid, 52.
688 Ibid, 52-53.
689 Ibid, 53.
690 Ibid, 53.
691 Ibid, 53.
692 Ibid, 54.
693 Ibid, 54.
694 Ibid, 54-55.
695 Ibid, 55.
696 Ibid, 55.
697 Ibid, 59.
698 Ibid, 59.
699 Ibid, 59-60.
700 Ibid, 60.
701 Ibid, 60.
702 Ibid, 60.
703 Ibid, 60.
704 Ibid, 61.
705 Ibid, 61.
706 Ibid, 61.
707 Shaw 1991, 43; Shaw & Boatright 2008, 40; Stonborough 2011, 61.
708 Stonborough 2011, 61-62.
709 Ibid, 62.
710 Hayes 1953, 278; Stonborough 2011, 62.
711 Stonborough 2011, 62.
712 Ibid, 62.
713 Ibid, 62.
714 Ibid, 62-63.
715 Ibid, 63.
716 Ibid, 63.
717 Ibid, 64.
718 Ibid, 64.
719 Filer 1992, 285, cited in Graves-Brown 2010.
720 Dean 2009.
721 Ibid.
722 Stonborough 2011, 65.
723 Ibid, 65.
724 Ibid, 65.

Weapons Trauma in Ancient Egypt

725 Winlock 2007, 1.
726 Ibid, 5.
727 Ibid, 7.
728 Ibid, 9.
729 McDermott 2004, 50.
730 Dean 2013, 214.
731 Winlock 2007, 14.
732 Ibid, 14.
733 Ibid, 15.
734 McDermott 2004, 51.
735 Winlock 2007, 15.
736 Ibid, 16.
737 Dean 2013, 215.
738 Winlock 2007, 16.
739 Dean 2013, 215.
740 Dean 2009, 38, 46.
741 McDermott 2004, 51.
742 Dean 2009, 216.
743 Winlock 2007; McDermott 2004.
744 Dean 2013, 216.
745 Ibid, 216.
746 Smith 2000, 1 [facsimile reprint of 1912 edition]; Shaw and Nicholson 1997, 260; Dean 2013, 217.
747 Shaw and Nicholson 1997, 260; Dean 2013, 217.
748 Smith 2000, 1; Dean 2013, 217.
749 Smith 2000, 2-1.
750 Ibid; Winlock 1924, 249; Dean 2013, 217.
751 Smith 2000, 2; Dean 2013, 217.
752 ten Berge and van de Goot 2002, 232; Dean 2013, 217.
753 Smith 2000, 2.
754 Ibid, 2; Dean 2013, 217-218.
755 Smith 2000, 2; Dean 2013, 218.
756 Smith 2000, 4; Dean 2013, 218.
757 Smith 2004, 4, Dean 2013, 218.
758 Smith 2000, 5.
759 Dean 2013, 218.
760 Smith 2000, 4.
761 Ibid, 4-5.
762 Smith 2000, 5; Dean 2013, 218.
763 Smith 2000, 5; Dean 2013, 218.
764 Dean 2013, 218.
765 Shaw and Nicholson 1997, 260.
766 Ibid, 260; Dean 2013, 221.
767 Smith 2000, 5.
768 Ibid, 5.
769 Dean 2009, 39; Dean 2013, 219.

770   Dean 2009, 39; Dean 2013, 219.
771   Smith 2000, 5; Dean 2013, 219.
772   Smith 2000, 5; Adams 1998, 35; ten Berge and van de Goot 2002, 232; Dean 2013, 219.
773   Smith 2000, 5.
774   Ibid, 5.
775   Ibid, 5; Winlock 1924, 249; Dean 2013, 220.
776   Dean 2013, 220.
777   Smith 2000, 6; Dean 2013, 220.
778   Smith 2000, 6; ten Berge and van de Goot 2002, 232.
779   Dean 2013, 221.
780   Smith 2000, 6; Dean 2013, 221.
781   Smith 2000, 6; Dean 2013, 221.
782   Smith 2000, 6.
783   Winlock 1924, 250.
784   Ibid, 250.
785   Shaw 2009, Abstract.
786   Ibid, Abstract.
787   Dean 2013, 222.
788   Dean 2009; Dean 2013.
789   Parsche *et al.* 1996, 326.
790   Ibid, 326.
791   Ibid, 326.
792   Ibid, 327.
793   Ibid, 327.
794   Ibid, 327.
795   Ibid, 327-328.
796   Ibid, 329.
797   Ibid, 331.
798   Ibid, 331.
799   Dean 2013, 224.
800   Ibid, 224.
801   Filer 1992, 282.
802   Ibid, 283.
803   Ibid, 283.
804   Ibid, 283.
805   Ibid, 283.
806   Ibid, 283.
807   Ibid, 283.
808   Ibid, 284.
809   Ibid, 285.
810   Pahor and Cole 1995, 273.
811   Ibid, 273.
812   Dr K. Dean, pers. comm. December 2012.
813   Pahor and Cole 1995, 274-275.
814   Ibid, 275.
815   Ibid, 275.
816   Ibid, 275.

817 Ibid, 275.
818 Dean 2013, 229.
819 Ibid, 229.
820 Erfan *et al.* 2009, 79.
821 Ibid, 79.
822 Ibid, 79; Dean 2013, 230.
823 Erfan *et al.* 2009, 82; Dean 2013, 230.
824 Erfan *et al.* 2009, 79; Dean 2013, 230-231.
825 Erfan *et al.* 2009, 80.
826 Dean 2013, 231.
827 Erfan *et al.* 2009, 82; Dean 2013, 231.
828 Erfan *et al.* 2009, 82.
829 Ibid, 82.
830 Ibid, 82.
831 Dean 2013, 232; Winlock 2007, 9.
832 Dean 2013, 232.

Conclusion
833 Wrobel 2004, 169.

Appendix
834 Gaunt 2011.
835 Dean 2009, 19.
836 Ibid.
837 Ibid.
838 Ibid, 20.
839 Ibid, 20; Fletcher 2007.
840 Dean 2009, 20.
841 Ibid, 20.
842 Ibid, 20; Fletcher 2007.
843 Dean 2009, 21.
844 Ibid, 21.
845 Dean 2009, 21; Fletcher 2007.
846 Dean 2009, 21; Fletcher 2007.
847 Dean 2009, 22.
848 Ibid; Fletcher 2007.
849 Dean 2009, 22.
850 Ibid; Fletcher 2007.
851 Dean 2009, 23; Fletcher 2007.
852 Dean 2009, 23.
853 Ibid, 23.
854 Dean 2009, 23; Fletcher 2007.
855 Dean 2009, 24; Fletcher 2007.
856 Dean 2009, 24.
857 Ibid, 24; Fletcher 2007.
858 Dean 2009 25; Fletcher 2007.
859 Dean 2009, 25.

860   Ibid, 25.
861   Dean 2009, 25; Fletcher 2007.
862   Dean 2009, 25.
863   Ibid, 25; Fletcher 2007.
864   Dean 2009, 26; Fletcher 2007.
865   Dean 2009, 26; Fletcher 2007.
866   Dean 2009, 26.
867   Ibid, 26.
868   Ibid, 26.
869   Dean 2009, 27.
870   Ibid, 27.
871   Ibid, 27.